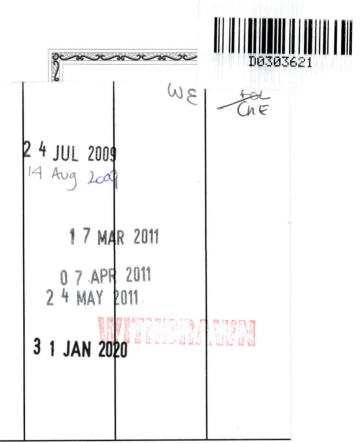

FDR and Lucy

LOVERS AND FRIENDS

Resa Willis

Routledge
Taylor & Francis Group
New York London

Routledge is an imprint of the
Taylor & Francis Group, an informa business

First paperback edi[illegible]

Routledge
Taylor & Francis Group
270 Madison Avenue
New York, NY 10016

Routledge
Taylor & Francis Group
2 Park Square
Milton Park, Abingdon
Oxon OX14 4RN

Routledge is an imprint of Taylor & Francis Group, an Informa business

Printed in the United States of America on acid-free paper
10 9 8 7 6 5 4 3 2 1

International Standard Book Number-10: 0-415-98013-5 (Softcover)
International Standard Book Number-13: 978-0-415-98013-5 (Softcover)
Library of Congress Card Number 2004011760

Library of Congress Cataloging-in-Publication Data

Willis, Resa.
FDR and Lucy: lovers and friends/Resa Willis.
p. cm.
Includes bibliographical references and index.
ISBN 0-415-98013-5 (softcover: acid-free paper)
1. Roosevelt, Franklin D. (Franklin Delano), 1882–1945—Friends and associates. 2. Roosevelt, Franklin D. (Franklin Delano), 1882–1945—Relations with women. 3. Rutherfurd, Lucy Mercer. 4. Presidents—United States—Biography. 5. Social secretaries—United States—Biography. I. Title: Franklin Delano Roosevelt and Lucy. II. Title.

E807.W565 2004
973.917'092'2—dc22 2004011760

Visit the Taylor & Francis Web site at
http://www.taylorandfrancis.com

and the Routledge Web site at
http://www.routledge-ny.com

This book is dedicated to
my family members, some living, some deceased,
who belong to the World War II generation to whom we owe
so much. My husband's parents, Richard and Edith Willis,
won the war in England. My father-in-law served King George VI
in Europe. My mother-in-law still lives in Essex.

My parents, Lawrence and Hazel Holsapple, won the war
in Iowa on their farm. My sisters, Edith and Janyce, won
the war by dancing with soldiers at the USO. They married
two men who won the war in the Pacific, my brothers-in-law,
respectively, Harold Reynolds and James Hall. Jim now
lives in Omaha.

My neighbors and relatives, Harley and Lucille Reynolds,
won the war, too, Harley by driving for General Patton and
Lucille by working on the home front. She still lives
in Missouri.

CONTENTS

ACKNOWLEDGMENTS

Franklin Roosevelt once joked that he could tell his life to a prospective biographer in fourteen and a half minutes. Eleanor Roosevelt wanted to write up her life for her children. It took her eight books. If Lucy recorded any portion of her own life story, historians haven't found it, but we keep hoping.

The best thing about biography is the wonderful people you meet along the way during your research. At the Franklin Delano Roosevelt Presidential Library in Hyde Park, New York, I'm grateful to Karen Anson, Bob Clark, Robert Parks, Raymond Teichman, Mark Renovitch, and Alycia Vivona. My thanks go also to the former director of the library, Verne Newton, and the present director, Cynthia Koch. All of them answered my questions and skillfully guided me toward sources and areas I might have overlooked.

At Warm Springs, Georgia, Mary Thrash is a fountain of knowledge concerning Roosevelt's years there. The Aiken Historical Society in South Carolina provided background information on that area Lucy so loved, as did the New Jersey Historical Society on Allamuchy.

At Margaret "Daisy" Suckley's home of Wilderstein in Rhinebeck, New York, Duane and Linda Watson have done so much to increase the knowledge of Franklin Roosevelt by making the journals and letters of Miss Suckley available to scholars.

The librarians at my university were always ready to answer questions, find books, and nudge me sympathetically when those books were overdue.

Every biographer builds upon the foundation set by others. Any errors are of my making and not of those whose research and writings I've depended upon. A glance at my bibliography only gives a reader an inkling of how many people have been fascinated by Franklin and Eleanor Roosevelt, and now, Lucy Rutherfurd. I am grateful that I crossed paths with Ellen Feldman, the author of the novel *Lucy*. She shared her discoveries with me in such a gracious manner. Several years ago in the midst of my biography of Olivia Langdon Clemens, Mark Twain's wife, I was thinking of the next book. Geoffrey Ward encouraged me in my pursuit to learn more about Lucy. The late Bernard Asbell recommended that I also look closely at the other women around Roosevelt, for he did seem to have a talent in attracting women who were willing to devote their lives to him. Jon Meacham kindly talked with me of his discoveries about Lucy.

I wish to thank Lucy Mercer Blunden and her husband Montague for inviting me into their home. Working on this project has reinforced for me how the Rutherfurd family treasures their memories of Lucy.

My agent Elaine Markson is always willing to handle the business details so I can concentrate on my writing. I'm grateful to Ron Longe for directing me toward Routledge and to my two editors there, Karen Wolny and Jaclyn Bergeron.

ACKNOWLEDGMENTS

Biography is a strange art. It requires the writer to forfeit his or her life in order to concentrate on others. You ignore facts of your own family history in favor of chasing down details of someone else's. I couldn't write about the lives of others without the people in my own life. On my days of uncertainty, I'm fortunate to have people around me who never doubt me. In my family, they are my husband, Michael, and my niece Theresa. From my friends, they are Katherine Kurk, Krystal Compas, Eltjen Flikkema, and Stephen Good.

Finally, there are the people who work hard to make me look good. I know it's not easy for J.D. Dunning, George Mires, or Dr. Jerry Cash and his staff.

INTRODUCTION

My father, an Iowa farmer, was a Democrat, but not any old Democrat. He was a Roosevelt Democrat. He believed we would have first "starved to death" during the Depression and second would "be speaking Japanese or German" after World War II without Franklin Delano Roosevelt. He liked to talk about how he had actually seen FDR speak from the back of his campaign train in Onawa, Iowa during 1932 when Roosevelt was running for president the first time. His story always ended with the same words, "He was a wealthy man; he was a powerful man. I don't know why he couldn't have found himself a better looking woman." He was referring, of course, to Eleanor Roosevelt whom he actually admired as a humanitarian. In those pre–politically correct days, he thought nothing of saying such a thing in front of my mother and his impressionable daughter.

What my dad didn't know then, nor did the American public, was that there was another woman whom Franklin Roosevelt had loved since 1914. She attended all of his inaugurations and visited him often in the White House. She was with him at

Warm Springs when he died in 1945. Her name was Lucy Mercer Rutherfurd.

The details of her relationship with Franklin Roosevelt took years to become known. In 1949 Roosevelt's secretary Grace Tully mentioned in her book *F.D.R., My Boss* that Mrs. Winthrop Rutherfurd had accompanied the artist Elizabeth Shoumatoff to Warm Springs. Shoumatoff was painting Roosevelt's portrait when he died. In the days following the president's death, when Shoumatoff was answering questions about what had transpired, she did not reveal Lucy's name as Lucy had wished.

Rumors circulated. In the multitude of books published by those in the Roosevelt circle in the ten years after his death, discretion prevailed probably out of respect for Eleanor. Even Michael Reilly, FDR's Secret Service guard, removed all mention of Lucy Rutherfurd from his detailed logs before publishing them. Former White House press secretary Jonathan Daniels felt "such a great romantic story in history will not be long hid." He approached Anna Roosevelt Halsted, the only daughter of Franklin and Eleanor Roosevelt, late in 1963. The story of her father and Lucy should be written. The three principals were now all dead. Eleanor was the last, dying in 1962. Anna was reluctant, "I feel that those who did not love him . . . will do everything possible to sensationalize a story such as this in a very negative way, no matter how beautifully it is written." She wanted Daniels to write it but felt, "the story should be put under lock and key for 20 to 25 years."

By 1966 Anna was realizing that, "I know you must write about the affection between Father and Lucy Mercer Rutherford [*sic*]; others will, too, of course; and I have no doubt that your writing will be truthful, not hearsay, and sympathetic, not sensational."

In 1966, Daniels published his book *The Time between the Wars* in which he mentions the romance of Lucy and FDR. At sixteen, I was intrigued with this love story. My father, then in the last year of his life, and along with much of the country, simply wouldn't believe it. When Daniels elaborated on their story in *Washington*

Quadrille in 1968, the furor began. Anna felt compelled to comment on the romance in several articles she started but never published. In one she writes, "One cannot help wonder whether preoccupation with sensation involving private aspects of living is not one of the devastatingly bad features of the American civilization, something immature, undignified and unbecoming a people who may be destined for greatness." Friends and family of Lucy Mercer Rutherfurd came to her defense. Her neighbors in her winter home of Aiken, South Carolina, refused to believe Daniels. Lucy's daughter, Barbara, stated Roosevelt and her mother "were good friends, but to call it a romance is going rather far."

The Roosevelt children had to address the love triangle in their various books on their parents. James stated, "Yet, if father loved Lucy, as I suppose he did, I do not believe he loved mother any the less of it. I think of his long affair with Lucy as beautiful, not ugly." Anna reported that while she knew of their past, when Lucy came into her father's life again, "Never was there anything clandestine about these occasions." Elliott gave a very thorough, journalistic accounting of his father's relationship with Lucy. Franklin Delano Roosevelt, Jr. stated, "My mother . . . and my father had a beautiful and ideal life together." Yet, Eleanor admitted of her husband, "He might have been happier with a wife who was completely uncritical. That I was never able to be, and he had to find it in other people."

The debate goes on as to whether FDR and Lucy did or didn't physically consummate their love when they were first attracted to each other and when Roosevelt was in the White House. We may never know, but it doesn't matter. They loved each other on various levels of intensity for thirty years. Lucy was a part of Franklin Roosevelt's life during a crucial time in our country's history. Her entry into the life of Eleanor Roosevelt changed Eleanor forever and did much to turn her into the tireless public servant she became.

Yet, this book is more than a love story involving Franklin, Lucy, and Eleanor. It's also about the other people drawn to these three charismatic individuals.

CHAPTER 1

"While I am alive"

Lucy Mercer Rutherfurd lay awake most of the night of Wednesday, April 11, 1945, in the guesthouse of the Little White House in Warm Springs, Georgia. Worry about the health of the man she once yearned to marry, Franklin Delano Roosevelt, now the thirty-second President of the United States, kept her from sleeping. She knew the look of death; she had become a widow just the previous year.

"Inexorably drawn to each other," was how Lucy described herself and FDR. They first met in 1914 when she was a twenty-three-year-old single, attractive woman whose prominent family had fallen on hard times. Eleanor Roosevelt, pregnant for the fifth time in eight years, hired her to help with the increasing Washington social duties that befell the wife of the assistant secretary of the navy. When Eleanor discovered their affair in 1918, she agreed to step aside so that her husband could marry Lucy, but FDR's mother, Sara Delano Roosevelt, threatened to "not give him another dollar." A divorce and remarriage to a Catholic would ruin her son's political career. Although in love, Lucy and

Franklin vowed they would never have contact again. Yet, over thirty years later, Roosevelt looked into this "smiling face of a beautiful woman" before he died.

April 12, 1945, dawned a warm, sticky Georgia morning. The elevation of the pine-covered mountains of Warm Springs alleviated some of the heat. Franklin Roosevelt, a sufferer of poliomyelitis, had visited the restorative waters since 1924 to ease the symptoms of the disease that struck him in 1921. Over the years, he bought an old resort, farmland, woods, and established the Georgia Warm Springs Foundation and the National Foundation for Infantile Paralysis. In the spring of 1932, "The Little White House," as he named it before he was even elected governor of New York in 1928, was completed on the north slope of Pine Mountain.

In the Georgia woods, with the therapy of the natural warm waters and the simplicity of his six-room home, Roosevelt found he could relax from the cares of his presidency—first the Great Depression and the New Deal, and then the burdens of World War II. He had last been in Warm Springs in December 1944, and as was the practice when Eleanor wasn't around, so was Lucy.

Roosevelt returned by train on March 30, 1945, in need of a physical and emotional rest. Photographs taken in February at the Yalta conference where he, Churchill, and Stalin discussed a postwar world show his physical deterioration. Cardiologist Dr. Howard Bruenn, alarmed at Roosevelt's high blood pressure, his pale, gray complexion, and the tremor in his hands, ordered total rest. Dr. Bruenn, Roosevelt's cousins Laura "Polly" Delano, Margaret "Daisy" Suckley, and Grace Tully, his secretary, accompanied him on the journey. Bruenn limited Roosevelt to seeing minimal staff and a few friends.

At the top of the list of old friends was Lucy Mercer Rutherfurd. Anna Roosevelt Boettiger, the president's daughter, had been scheduled to accompany the group south when her six-year-old son was hospitalized. Knowing how her father enjoyed Lucy's company but unknown to her mother, Anna arranged, as she had done in the past, for Lucy to visit her father in Warm Springs.

Roosevelt looked forward to Lucy's visit, for he called her daily at her home in Aiken, South Carolina. They had last seen each other in March when Lucy stayed with her sister in Georgetown for a week. Again, Anna arranged to bring Lucy to the White House while Eleanor was speaking in North Carolina. "I was grateful to her," Anna said because Lucy's presence allowed her father a respite.

In the two weeks since he had seen Lucy, Franklin worked hard to improve his appearance. When he first arrived in Warm Springs, a train station employee described him as "the worst looking man I ever saw who was still alive." His Secret Service chief, Mike Reilly, who had lifted the president countless times into and out of automobiles, found him on this occasion to be total "dead weight." At six-feet-two-inches tall and having lost around thirty pounds, FDR was sensitive about looking thin. The good weather, rest, relaxation, warm springs, and good food brought color back to his cheeks for Lucy's arrival.

After several hours drive from Aiken, she arrived the early evening of Monday, April 9, with her friend, the artist Elizabeth Shoumatoff, who was to paint a portrait of the president for Lucy's daughter Barbara Rutherfurd, a young woman in her early twenties. To help with the portrait Shoumatoff brought the photographer Nicholas Robbins.

Lucy found Roosevelt thin but still handsome. "There is something about his face that shows more the way he looked when he was young," she told Shoumatoff. Perhaps with a sense of foreboding Lucy stressed that the painting of a second portrait of the president "should not be postponed." Lucy had first commissioned Elizabeth to paint a portrait of the president for her in 1943. "He has such a remarkable face. There is no painting of him that gives his true expression. I think you could do a wonderful portrait, and he would be such an interesting person to paint!"

Roosevelt reserved mornings for the presidential business of studying official papers, reading and answering letters, and writing speeches. Lizzie McDuffie, the maid, carried breakfast trays the hundred feet from the Little White House to the two-room guesthouse behind it. Guests entertained themselves after breakfast by walking through the woods among the azaleas. Fala, the president's gregarious Scottie, who had been a present from Daisy Suckley, liked to toddle down the walkway to bid guests good morning. On occasion, he could be persuaded to do tricks of jumping, speaking, lying down, or begging, at which he was particularly adept. Indeed, Fala took seriously his ceremonial duties as first dog. He had been president of the Barkers for Britain campaign to send aid to the bombed out victims of Germany's blitz against England in the days prior the United States entering the war.*

All guests, including the occasional visiting dignitary, joined Roosevelt for lunch. The president of the Philippines, Sergio Osmena, had visited the previous Thursday on April 5 to discuss the war in the Pacific and his nation's future independence. Leighton McCarthy, the former minister to Canada, lunched with the group on April 10.

Roosevelt devoted his afternoons to napping, working on his stamp collection, chatting with his guests, and driving around the countryside. It was in Georgia that FDR regained the freedom of operating an automobile despite his paralyzed legs. He sketched controls for a car that allowed him to operate a clutch, brake, and accelerator with his hands. A local mechanic named Ponder first adapted the design to a Model T Ford and later to other vehicles.

*The definitive biography of Fala is *The True Story of Fala* by Margaret L. Suckley and Alice Dalgliesh, 1942.

Roosevelt so liked having a car he could operate in Warm Springs that he had one made for his Hyde Park, New York, home as well. The ability to drive allowed Roosevelt, a man dependent on others for mobility, to escape the Secret Service to be on his own or with Lucy for afternoon drives and picnics. Daisy recorded just such a drive on Wednesday, April 11, in her diary. She described Lucy and FDR together. "Lucy is so sweet with F—no wonder he loves to have her around." When it got chilly, Lucy placed her sweater over Roosevelt's knees, which prompted Daisy to write, "I can imagine just how she took care of her husband—she would think of *little* things which make so much difference to a semi-invalid, or even a person who is just *tired*, like F."

As the day wound down, the president served late afternoon cocktails in front of the stone fireplace in the combination living, dining room, and president's office on an old card table that served as his workspace in the morning. At dinner, all guests ate with the president. Lucy sat to his right as FDR held court. Much of Franklin's initial attraction to the still beautiful woman, who would turn fifty-four in a few weeks, was that, as Anna recalled, "Lucy was a wonderful listener." Unlike Eleanor who debated with her husband, Lucy was content to listen adoringly, waiting to ask the "right questions." Feminine, intelligent, with her "Mona Lisa smile," she quietly observed and evaluated those doing all the talking. Despite Lucy's willingness to acquiesce, Elliott Roosevelt, the president's second eldest son, acknowledged something deeper, "There was a hint of fire in her warm dark eyes."

Daisy who had known Lucy from her early days in Aiken thought her "lovely" but "immature—like a character out of a book." Daisy attributed this to the sheltered, affluent life her late husband had provided for her. "Now, she faces a very different future, rather alone. . . ." Roosevelt had confided to Daisy that Lucy, "has *so many* problems & difficulties that she brings to him.

She has no other person like him—a friend of such long standing—to whom to go for the kind of sympathetic understanding which he always gives."

Shoumatoff felt that "in the presence of FDR you experienced ease and relaxation" as he told jokes and lead the conversation on topics that varied from the idiosyncrasies of world leaders to the local peach crop. He could imitate Churchill and he called Stalin "a jolly fellow." At Dr. Bruenn's nudging, Roosevelt retired early leaving his guests to move closer to the fireplace for more conversation. Often the president of the United States would "beg like a kid" to stay up a bit longer.

Lucy reiterated her concerns for Roosevelt's health to her friend Shoumatoff, "He really should have a male nurse or somebody to take care of him. He has an excellent doctor but that is not enough. His general health has been failing ever since his last campaign. He did entirely too much but he felt that he could not leave his post at that time."

Shoumatoff was in the habit of starting each morning by reading a passage from the Christian publication the *Daily Word*. She usually shared these daily aphorisms to keep faith, hope, and to work hard with Lucy, but on the morning of April 12, she did not reveal the maxim advising the reader to have no fear despite foreboding circumstances and disastrous events.

As scheduled each day of her visit, Shoumatoff set up to begin work on her portrait of the president around noon. She and the president had decided she would paint him in his cape holding a rolled piece of paper, an old program from a Jefferson Day dinner. FDR was working on the speech for this year's dinner, scheduled for April 13. Some suggested it could signify the peace treaty. Roosevelt said that no, but "the United Nations Charter!" He was planning to attend the San Francisco conference, which would draft the charter later in the month. The background of the portrait was to be plain as advocated by Lucy, Polly, and

Daisy although they first had to dissuade the president from choosing Hyde Park.

Shoumatoff did not feel like painting that day, for she had heard the previous day that her brother had suffered a heart attack. She found the president with his assistant William Hassett surrounded by his "laundry" as he called the mass of papers on which the ink was drying from his signature. Despite her offer to postpone the sitting until the next day, Roosevelt stated, "Oh, no, I'll be through in a few moments and will be ready for you."

Lucy and Daisy, who was crocheting, sat on a sofa talking with FDR while Elizabeth set up her easel near the open door of the porch to catch the light. Roosevelt sat behind the multipurpose card table strewn with papers that distracted his attention. From time to time Shoumatoff had to ask him to look up or get him engaged in talking about stamps. Lucy and Daisy chatted with him about his busy schedule that day. He was still working on his Jefferson Day speech, he was due to attend a barbecue hosted by the Warm Springs mayor, and he planned to take Lucy for an afternoon drive. The countryside and the company were working their magic on his health. Shoumatoff noted, "That gray look had disappeared." Daisy found him "smiling & happy & ready for anything." Lizzie McDuffie, the president's maid, on her way to make the beds in the guest cottage saw Roosevelt talking and laughing with Lucy. "The last I remember he was looking into the smiling face of a beautiful woman."

Prior to lunch Roosevelt had already swallowed a green concoction and ate some of Daisy's gruel, both of which were to increase his appetite. Lucy had brought Dextrin with her as she had given it to her ailing husband to help his appetite. Dr. Bruenn advised Daisy that he would only use it if the president kept losing weight. When the butler entered and began to set the table, Roosevelt told him that they had "fifteen minutes more to work." According to Shoumatoff, these were his last words. He busied himself with the papers on the card table. Others reported that he remarked that he had a headache, but Shoumatoff recounts that he passed his right hand in jerky motions several times across his forehead and collapsed unconscious into his chair. It was around 1:15 P.M.

Daisy Suckley's account differs slightly, or as she states in her journal, "Mme. S. has given *her* version. . . . She then writes. *My* version is as follows." Daisy noticed "F seemed to be looking for something: his head forward, his hands fumbling. . . . 'Have you dropped your cigarette?'" she asked. Roosevelt said he had "a terrific pain" in the back of his head. While she heard him say this, she did acknowledge that his voice was low, and she was close to him so she may have been the only person to hear it. Because he had slumped forward, Polly and Lucy tilted and held his chair back as Daisy telephoned Dr. Bruenn. Madame Shoumatoff went to find help. She found Arthur Prettyman, the president's valet, and Joe Esperancilla, the Filipino butler, who picked up Roosevelt while Polly held his feet. They carried him into the bedroom. Polly Delano would later say she heard the president say, "Be careful." She also recalled that he looked at all of them, but Daisy saw no "real recognition in those eyes." Lucy passed camphor under his nose. In a short time, which seemed an eternity, the doctor arrived. "We must pack and go," Lucy said to her friend Elizabeth Shoumatoff. "The family is arriving by plane and the rooms must be vacant. We must get to Aiken before dark."

Lucy and Elizabeth went to the guest cottage and began throwing things into suitcases. The maid Lizzie wept as she helped them pack. Daisy cried and talked of the ghost stories they had told the previous evenings and their talk of reincarnation. An army car arrived with Mr. Robbins who had been in town eating lunch.

Grace Tully accompanied them as their luggage was carried to Shoumatoff's white Cadillac convertible. With Elizabeth Shoumatoff driving, Lucy next to her, and a bewildered Robbins in the back, the three left the Little White House around 2:30 in the afternoon. Lucy cried quietly until they went through Greenville where the president had just met them four days earlier. Lucy asked for the exact corner where he had sat in his car, and Robbins pointed it out. When Robbins questioned their hasty departure, Lucy replied that she had received bad news about her oldest stepson who had been wounded.

By the time they approached Macon, they saw the flag at half-mast. Lucy asked to stop at a hotel to call home and Warm Springs. She reached her daughter in Aiken, but all lines to Warm Springs were busy. Shoumatoff went to the main switchboard to find an operator to put through a call and heard the operators crying that the president was dead. She returned to the lobby where Lucy sat silently. "The expression on her pale face was more eloquent than words."

Mr. Robbins approached them and on hearing, "He is dead," from Elizabeth thought she was speaking of Lucy's stepson.

They left the hotel and drove on in silence when Lucy suggested they turn on the radio. H. V. Kaltenborn, the news commentator, spoke of the death of the president and erroneously stated that an architect was making sketches when the president was stricken. In shock, Lucy alternately began rambling about everything and anything and crying. Robbins who had remained in ignorance of the events until hearing it on the radio blurted out, "Why didn't you tell me?"

With Robbins driving and the women talking in the back seat, they reached Aiken around midnight after taking the wrong road, which put them eighty miles out of their way.

Robbins and Shoumatoff then headed north. In the dark, they stopped at a railway crossing as the funeral train with FDR's body passed on its way to Washington, D.C.

Shoumatoff feared the notoriety that would come when it was discovered that she was present at Roosevelt's death. Pursued by the press, she finally held a press conference and as per Lucy's request, did not mention her name. The two friends met a few months later in June. It was then Lucy announced, "I have burned all his letters." Shoumatoff informed her friend, "I have it all written down, because in the years to come it should be known the way it was."

Lucy's response was, "I don't mind what you have written because I trust you, but I do not wish anything to be brought out while I am alive!" For a while, Lucy Mercer Rutherfurd got her wish and disappeared into history.

CHAPTER 2

"Rich in heritage if not funds"

Children of the Gilded Age, Lucy Mercer and Franklin Roosevelt were both born into wealth and privilege at the end of the nineteenth century. Their ancestors had lived and prospered on the eastern seaboard of the United States for hundreds of years. Lucy's paternal family, the Mercers, descended from the Catholics who under the second Lord Baltimore had settled Chesapeake Bay and founded Maryland in the 1630s.

At about this same time, Claes Martenszen Van Rosenvelt, the common ancestor of Franklin Roosevelt, Theodore Roosevelt, and his niece, Eleanor, arrived in New York City and became a successful merchant. Roosevelt's mother, Sara Delano, felt her lineage was even more distinguished. She liked to tell anyone who'd listen that the Delano line went back to William the Conqueror. On the western side of the Atlantic, Delanos were among the settlers of the Massachusetts Bay Colony in 1621 and leaders in maritime commerce.

Both Mercers and Roosevelts could point to forbears who had taken part in the founding of the country. The Mercers gave their name to Mercersburg, Maryland. Lucy's father was named Carroll Mercer to represent both sides of his family. The state song "Maryland, My Maryland!" has the line, "Remember Carroll's sacred trust." Carrolls and Mercers sent representatives to the Second Continental Congress. They could brag that Charles Carroll of Carrollton was not only the sole Catholic signer of the Declaration of Independence but also the only signer wealthier than George Washington. Carroll's brother became the first American Catholic Archbishop. By the American Revolution, the name Rosenvelt had become Roosevelt, and the family made money as sugar refiners. Isaac Roosevelt (1726–1794) served at the Constitutional ratification convention, was one of the first New York state senators, and a president of the Bank of New York.

The Hudson River Valley became home to the Roosevelts in the nineteenth century when FDR's great-grandfather built a home near Poughkeepsie. James Roosevelt, Franklin's father, purchased one hundred acres and a house called Springwood at Hyde Park overlooking the Hudson River in 1866. It was here that Franklin Roosevelt was born January 30, 1882. His entire life he regarded this area as his only home. "All that is within me cries out to go back to my home on the Hudson River," he often said.

The area attracted the wealthy. Frederick William Vanderbilt, grandson of "Commodore" Cornelius Vanderbilt, the richest man in America in his time, would build a mansion down the road from Springwood in 1895 as a retreat from his yacht, his New York City townhouse, and his home at Newport.

Lucy's grandfather John Tunis also knew the value of real estate to the rich for he became wealthy selling land along the mid-Atlantic to them. Lucy's grandmother Caroline came from the distinguished Hendersons of North Carolina. Lucy's mother, Minnie Tunis, was born in Norfolk, Virginia, on June 18, 1863.

By the time she was a young woman in Norfolk, Minnie or Minna, as she was christened, was a dark beauty who could choose from any young man who traveled in her social circle. When she was twenty, in 1883, her father died and she married Percy Norcop, an Englishman who helped her spend her inherited fortune. She divorced him for adultery in 1886. She consoled herself by traveling among her relations in North Carolina and by having a home near Dupont Circle in Washington described as "so rich and beautiful it strikes everyone who comes in."

Minnie had already met Carroll Mercer in 1883. Her future second husband had the same playboy appeal of the first. Born in Washington, D.C., in 1858, he spent his time at parties and as a riding, shooting, gaming sportsman until his father's death, but his physician father did not leave him enough money to maintain those activities. What is a young gentleman without suitable education or training to do? Through family connections at the age of twenty-three, Mercer got his commission as a lieutenant in the U.S. Marines. He served three years in the Philippines. In April 1885, while in Panama, he was too drunk for duty, and he was suspended on half pay for two years. His suspension was lifted in 1886.

By 1887 Minnie and Carroll were engaged. They made a handsome couple for a society reporter called Minnie "the most beautiful woman in Washington." Minnie described her husband as "an inch over six feet . . . of fair complexion . . . blonde hair and grayish eyes. . . ." Minnie sailed for Europe on June 20, 1888, with her cousin Sallie Hoke to meet Carroll stationed on a gunboat anchored on the Thames. She had just turned twenty-five and declared, "This is my birthday, my last one. . . ."

In London, Minnie inadvertently ran into her former mother-in-law; neither spoke. "She certainly does look hateful," Sallie wrote. The lovers' plan to marry was delayed because Minnie did not bring her divorce papers with her, and she didn't know where they were. Sallie prompted, "I think it is in the wooden box in the garret." Just as Minnie's letter of credit was running out, the copy of the divorce arrived. Minnie Tunis and Carroll Mercer were married off Trafalgar Square at St. Martin-in-the-Fields on July 30, 1888.

Mercer's ship, the *Quinnebaugh*, sailed from London to Constantinople and then on to Alexandria, Egypt. Minnie, now a sailor's wife, followed the ship seeing her husband at Liverno, Italy, and in Alexandria. After being married for just three months, she was pregnant. Money was already becoming a problem early in the marriage, for Mercer wired Minnie's lawyers asking for the total value of his wife's estate.

The *Quinnebaugh* docked at Alexandria from November 1888 to April 1889. The European-American colony in Alexandria flourished with expatriates and military personnel frequenting parties, galleries, and theaters. Minnie and Carroll went on sight-seeing expeditions to the sphinx and the pyramids. Violetta, their first child—named for Carroll's mother—was born March 31, 1889. Mercer sailed on the *Quinnebaugh* on April 10. Minnie started back to the United States with her new baby in June.

By June of the following year, Carroll resigned his commission to settle with his wife and daughter at Minnie's Washington home at 1744 P Street. There they pursued the life of "cave dwellers," a local term to designate native-born Washingtonians of a certain blue-blooded social strata. They formalized this distinction by establishing a Cave Dwellers Club. Minnie rode about town in a large horse drawn brougham with a liveried coachman and footman. She loved her reputation of being a once divorced, remarried woman in a time when to be divorced was to be a social outcast. She further shocked the older, more conservative members of society by smoking in public in an era when women didn't smoke. Despite these self-imposed handicaps, her beauty and vibrant personality allowed her to move through Washington society. *The Clubfellow and Washington Mirror* wrote of her, "to be invited to one of her dinners was in itself a social distinction that qualified one for admission to any home."

While his wife was riding about in her carriage, Carroll Mercer pursued his life as a "gentleman" as he now stated his occupation to be. He belonged to the best clubs—the exclusive Metropolitan Club, where Franklin Roosevelt later liked to eat and drink, and the Riding Club. He also helped organize the Chevy Chase Club in Maryland, where Roosevelt would one day play golf. It was into this atmosphere and lifestyle of the "gay Nineties" that Lucy Page Mercer was born April 26, 1891. True to her parents' lifestyle she was delivered by a doctor, Henry D. Frey, who was listed in both the *Social Register* and *Who's Who in America*.

Like F. Scott Fitzgerald characters, Minnie and Carroll Mercer partied until the money was gone. Mercer's drinking became worse, and the two argued about their dwindling funds. A worsening economy accelerating towards the Panic of 1893 aggravated their money losses. The panic began when foreign investors sold their securities and withdrew them in gold, which depleted federal gold reserves and, thus, confidence. Without gold or confidence, the stock market crashed and the dominoes fell taking down banks and businesses. A simpler explanation of the Mercers' money problems came from a cousin of Minnie's—"Pooh, they just spent it!" Years later Lucy would describe her parents as "rich in heritage if not funds."

The Spanish-American War, which Theodore Roosevelt allegedly called, "not much of a war, but the only war we had," erupted in 1898. By 1899, Mercer, the former Marine Lieutenant, became an Army Captain and Commissary of Subsistence U.S. Volunteers in 1899. He served with Colonel Theodore Roosevelt and the Rough Riders, "in command of needs," at the only major engagement of the war, the Battle of San Juan Hill. Promoted to major, he received an honorable discharge on June 30, 1901. The Mercers' monetary problems necessitated a move into a more modest home at 1761 N Street in Washington.

Here Lucy's parents separated in 1903 when she was twelve years old. Once a Fitzgerald character, Minnie now became the inhabitant of an Edith Wharton novel. She was a woman with two daughters to support in a time, and of a social status, that forbade ladies from working. Social convention had never stopped her before, so Minnie and daughters moved to a comfortable New York apartment where she used her background and experience to become an "inside decorator" to those with sudden wealth but no social background.

Despite their diminished funds, Minnie educated her daughters in private schools and managed to give them, with some help from the Carroll relatives, the obligatory year abroad in 1909. Lucy's great aunt, the Austrian Countess Heussenstamm of Melk, was the former Agnes Carroll of Maryland. Lucy and Violetta studied at an Austrian convent on the Danube near the home of their aunt. Their class consisted of about twenty privileged young women. The two sisters, along with their classmates, wore school uniforms during their lessons and changed into peasant dresses for the novelty of it after classes. In a school were modesty was supreme—rules stated that students must even bathe in chemises—the nuns were surprised at the naiveté of Lucy and Violetta. The nuns disapproved of the frilly nightgowns the young women wore saying they looked like they belonged to prostitutes, but Violetta, aged twenty, and Lucy, eighteen, did not know what a prostitute was. The education of Lucy and Violetta mirrored that of all young ladies of this time—to train them to be good wives and devout Christians.

Minnie and Carroll returned separately to Washington, D.C. in 1912. While the local gossip rag *Town Topics* reported that the Mercers were reunited and "all goes well as a marriage bell," they did not live together, but they also did not divorce. Minnie worked for "an art establishment" decorating the homes of incoming congressmen with appropriate paintings. Mercer returned to the prestigious Riding Club this time as a manager, not as a member. Minnie chose to avoid contact with her husband, but her daughters visited him through his illnesses of diabetes and Bright's disease aggravated by his alcoholism.

Despite their parents' problems, the Mercer daughters were young ladies ready to make their way in the world, and young women of their social status had only transitory careers until they made good marriages. Violetta became a nurse and married the doctor with whom she worked. Lucy, by then twenty, found occasional work as a decorator through her mother, but it did not provide enough income for them.

Lucy's training, background, and knowledge of Washington, D.C. suited her well to become a social secretary, which brought her into the lives of Eleanor and Franklin Roosevelt.

CHAPTER 3

"Inexorably drawn to each other"

Woodrow Wilson rewarded Franklin Roosevelt's support of his successful 1912 presidential campaign by making him assistant secretary of the navy in 1913. It was an important appointment for an ambitious young politician, and there was a sentimental tie—Theodore Roosevelt had once held this post. The new job meant the young New York state senator must leave Albany for Washington, D.C.

When the Roosevelts moved to Washington in the fall of 1913, Franklin was thirty-one and Eleanor twenty-nine. They had been married eight years with three children: Anna born in 1906, James born in 1907, and Elliott born in 1910. A fourth child, Franklin, Jr., born in 1909, lived only seven and a half months. In 1914, Eleanor became pregnant with the second Franklin, Jr.

The demands of Washington society that her husband's new position entailed soon overwhelmed Eleanor. Her job was to get to know influential people and to keep her husband's name before those who might one day help his career. Protocol required that she make afternoon calls on the wives of Cabinet members, Supreme Court justices, congressional members, and other high-ranking Washington personnel. Visits could be brief or if the lady of the house was not at home, a calling card could be left, but it was still time-consuming and exhausting. Formal luncheons, teas, dinners, and dances were either given or attended. Invitations had to be acknowledged, sorted, accepted, or rejected with the appropriate correspondence for each step of the process. At first reluctant to have a social secretary, Eleanor realized "that it took me such endless hours to arrange my calling list, and answer and send invitations, that I finally engaged one for three mornings a week."

By 1914, and at the recommendation of her Auntie Bye, the older sister of her father Elliott and her uncle Theodore and someone she often turned to for advice, she hired Lucy Mercer.* Auntie Bye knew the Mercers and their family history for they had lived down the street from her in Washington in the same neighborhood where the young Roosevelt family now rented Auntie Bye's house at 1733 N Street near Dupont Circle.** In all probability, Auntie Bye would have informed her niece of the similarities the two women shared growing up with a charismatic but doomed father. Franklin and Eleanor were acquainted with the young woman, for Lucy and her family had attended "the same Washington parties." Eleanor needed help, and Lucy needed money, and she brought insider knowledge of Washington society "which she knew like the back of her slim hands." For

*James Roosevelt thought "Cousin Polly," Laura Delano, had recommended Lucy to his mother.

**After President McKinley's assassination in 1901, Theodore Roosevelt became the youngest president in history. Bamie's house became his "Little White House" until Ida McKinley had time to leave 1600 Pennsylvania Avenue. Only a twenty-minute walk from the White House, Theodore used it as a refuge during his White House years (Caroli, p. 117).

this she was paid thirty dollars a week, which would cover the rent at the Decatur Apartments where she lived with her mother and sister.

At twenty-three, Lucy was statuesque at five-feet-nine-inches tall and "a lady to her fingertips." Thick brown hair worn in an upswept Victorian style accented her blue eyes and framed her face envied by others for its milky, translucent perfect complexion. She smiled often and her laughter revealed a deep voice "of dark velvet." All of her life people remarked on her beauty and her charm. Her friend Eulalie Salley said years after Lucy's death, "I think she was the most beautiful woman I ever saw. It was a beauty the artist and the photographer didn't catch. Her beauty was in her expression and in her graceful manner." FDR immediately noticed this. Lucy arrived for work at about the same time Franklin departed to the Navy Department. Roosevelt would always doff his hat to her as he strolled past and proclaim in a booming voice, "Ah, the lovely Lucy."

Not only efficient at her job, Lucy got along well with the Roosevelt children as remembered by Elliott.

> She and Mother worked together in the living room—there was no other space available. Lucy would curl herself gracefully on the carpet, spreading out for sorting the letters, cards, bills and invitations that flowed in, prompted by Mother's calls. Lucy was gay, smiling and relaxed. We children welcomed the days she came to work.

Anna's childhood recollections were similar. "I remember feeling happy and admiring when I was greeted one morning at home by Miss Lucy Mercer. I knew that she sat at a desk and wrote on cards; and I knew that I liked her warm and friendly manner and smile. . . ."

Lucy even managed to charm Franklin's mother, Sara Delano. Elliot described his grandmother as a woman "who could be stinging in her remarks to and about people she did not care for. . . ."

As far as Lucy was concerned, Sara told her daughter-in-law that she "found only praise for her: 'She is *so* sweet and attractive and adores you, Eleanor.'"

Roosevelt's first mention of Lucy, soon after she was hired, is in a letter to Eleanor who had taken the children to their Campobello, New Brunswick, summer home in preparation for giving birth to Franklin Jr. As assistant secretary, his duties included inspection tours of naval yards. From one of these trips he hastily returns home to attend a round of luncheons, dinners, and receptions. "Arrived safely and came to the house and Albert telephoned Miss Mercer who came later and cleaned up."

Roosevelt described her as "well acquainted with the social obligations of an Assistant Secretary's wife." No longer another employee being contacted through the chauffeur, Lucy soon served as an extra to fill out the table at social functions and occasionally acted as hostess when Eleanor found herself too busy with the stresses of children, servants, and her increasing volunteer work as an American role in World War I loomed closer.

Lucy stated years later that from the beginning she and Franklin Roosevelt, nine years her senior, were "inexorably drawn to each other" with mutual feelings of fondness and admiration. They had similar temperaments as described by Elliott Roosevelt, "She had the same brand of charm as Father, and everybody who met her spoke of that. . . ."

The face Lucy found "remarkable" other women also admired. At the Navy Department, female clerical workers would stop to watch Roosevelt go by. In his mid-thirties, he was not only handsome, but also gregarious. He loved attention, being the life of the party, flirting and teasing. Eleanor had been attracted to his confident, outgoing personality during their courtship just as Franklin had valued her seriousness. Now their differences in personality began to strain their marriage. Their only daughter, Anna, once remarked, "You couldn't find two such different people as Mother and Father." Franklin's family, especially his mother, doted on him as a child, and he never lacked for love. Eleanor did not have this security growing up. Her mother nicknamed her "Granny" to describe her daughter's personality. Anna Hall Roosevelt was a society beauty, and she criticized her daughter's appearance fearing she'd never make her way in society. Eleanor's mother died when she was only eight, her father's alcoholism and subsequent death two years later only added to her loneliness and lack of confidence. Eleanor portrayed her childhood with these few words, "I never smiled."

There was no denying the Roosevelt marriage was fertile. They had known each other from childhood, endured a yearlong engagement as dictated by Franklin's mother, and married very much in love. Eleanor returned from her European honeymoon pregnant with Anna, the first of six pregnancies in ten years. The longest span between children was the four years between Elliott in 1910 and Franklin, Jr. in 1914. Now in 1916 she was pregnant with her last child, John. Elliott Roosevelt noted, as all the children commented on sometime during their lives, that his parents' method of birth control was separate bedrooms, not uncommon for this time.

> Mother had performed her austere duty in marriage, and five children were testimony to that. She wanted no more, but her blank ignorance about how to ward off pregnancy left her no choice other than abstinence. Her shyness and stubborn pride would keep her from seeking advice from a doctor or woman friend. She said as much to her only daughter when Sis had grown up. It quickly became the most tightly held secret that we five children ever shared and kept.

Following John's birth in 1916, Elliott records, "my parents never again lived together as husband and wife." Eleanor would one day describe sex to Anna as "an ordeal to be borne."

A marriage of nearly twelve years, a meddling mother, an exhausted wife, a dashing husband, and a beautiful, younger woman are a recipe for infidelity. Corinne Alsop, Eleanor's cousin, said years after those involved in this love triangle were dead, "Eleanor and Franklin were both smart and had produced many children and on the whole it was a good marriage but it lacked 'delicieux.' The affair with Lucy provided the danger and excitement that was missing from Franklin's life."

When flirtation and innuendo led to physical contact and turned to love between Franklin and Lucy will never be known. "Of course he was in love with her. So was every man who ever knew Lucy," said her friend Eulalie Salley. Lucy's cousin Elizabeth Cotten recognized, "She and Franklin were very much in love with each other."

CHAPTER 4

"Part of the family"

Europe had been embroiled in World War I for three years when the United States entered the war on April 6, 1917. The "war to end all wars" changed the lives of Americans forever as the nation left the Victorian era and moved toward the advances and challenges of the twentieth century. Yet, no matter what the global events, human nature keeps people mired in their own personal triumphs and troubles, and thus it was for Lucy Mercer and for Franklin and Eleanor Roosevelt.

The war cut down on social obligations, and Lucy's work in the Roosevelt household. Knitting socks, washcloths, and scarves for American "doughboys" soon replaced Lucy's correspondence duties on behalf of Eleanor to Washington's society. Serving soup and coffee to soldiers at the Red Cross canteen in Union Station meant more to Eleanor's social conscience than presiding over a tea in her own drawing room. "I just loved it," Eleanor said years later. As part of the Comforts Committee of the Navy League, Eleanor and Lucy distributed free wool, so others could help in knitting clothing for soldiers "over there" in the trenches. Lucy's sister, Violetta

Mercer, was going to France as a Red Cross nurse. Washington society women formed a Patriotic Economy League and signed pledges to dress simply and save food as part of the war effort.

Franklin's duties at the Navy Department had grown steadily as the war advanced in Europe and then involved America. He became one of the Washington *"bachelors"* who stayed behind as wives and families left to avoid the oppressive heat of the capital summers. Lucy kept the household going in Washington and assisted Franklin with his correspondence for a while.

The first hint that Eleanor suspected more than an employer-and-employee relationship between her husband and her social secretary comes during this period. She writes to her husband from Campobello, July 1916, that she has heard from Lucy, "She tells me you are going off for Tuesday and I hope you all had a pleasant trip but I'm so glad I've been here and not on the Potomac!" An assistant secretary of the navy had access to ships, and Eleanor was speaking of trips on the Potomac River made under the auspices of naval business that were also yachting parties with friends.

Because of the polio epidemic in the northeastern United States, she stayed on with the children at Campobello until October. Twenty years later she wrote, "I went back to Washington from a life centered entirely in my family, I became conscious, on returning to the seat of government in Washington, that there was a sense of impending disaster hanging over all of us." Scholars have interpreted this as a reference to the war, but she was probably thinking of tragedy within her own family.

Elliott Roosevelt recalled an incident between his parents during this time that for him was an indication of the troubles within their marriage. Tucking him into bed, his mother began to weep, when questioned by her husband, she responded, "I can't bear to go down and meet our dinner guests. I'm afraid I cannot face all those people, Franklin." Roosevelt's response was "Do pull yourself together," perpetuating the upbringing in their families and of this time to never confront and openly speak of a problem.

Another often-repeated story of this era to illustrate Franklin's joie de vivre and Eleanor's insecurities and their inability to address the growing gulf in their marriage comes from Irene and Warren Delano Robbins. Cousins, friends, and former neighbors, they came to Washington to attend a dinner and private ball at the exclusive Chevy Chase Club. Eleanor left the ball before midnight saying she did not feel like dancing. The other three arrived home at dawn to find her sitting on the doormat locked out of the house. Perturbed, Franklin inquired why she hadn't returned to the dance to get his key. She replied, "I knew you were all having such a *glorious time,* and I didn't want to *spoil the fun.*" Of course, Lucy had been present at the dance.

When a chauffeur wrecked their car, Eleanor wrote her husband a message heavily infused with double meaning, "Isn't it horrid to be disappointed in someone? It makes one so suspicious!"

By the summer of 1917, she was reluctant to leave her husband behind in Washington with Lucy. Eleanor uncharacteristically joined one of his parties on the navy yacht *Sylph,* the smaller of two presidential yachts, on Saturday, June 16. The *Sylph* had served the presidents William McKinley, Theodore Roosevelt, and William Taft.

Lucy Mercer and the man who often acted as her date on these excursions, Nigel Law, the third secretary of the British Embassy, were two of the eight passengers. Law never minded being Lucy's escort, for he described Roosevelt as "a man I loved and admired," and "the most attractive man whom it was my fortune to meet during my four years in America." The deception fooled the gossip sheet *Town Topics* for it reported that an engagement would come soon. Eleanor was not so easily duped.

A week after the excursion and in an attempt to keep Lucy and FDR apart, Eleanor informed Lucy that because of the war and reduced social obligations she no longer needed her help. Lucy promptly enlisted in the navy in June as a female yeoman, to perform secretarial duties in the Navy Department. She and Franklin would still see each other every day as he had her assigned to his office. There seemed to be no keeping the two apart.

When Eleanor delayed taking the children to Campobello, she and Franklin argued. She hesitated but finally went north in July. In guilt, Roosevelt wrote his wife as soon as she left calling her a "goosy girl to think or even pretend to think that I don't want you here *all* summer, because you know I do!" In reality, he wanted more time with Lucy.

In the midst of this marital tension, another incident further frayed their nerves. The *New York Times* had interviewed Eleanor on the "food-saving program adopted at the home" of the assistant secretary of the navy as a model for other large households in the war conscious country. The article, "How to Save in Big Homes," appeared on July 17, just after she had left for Campobello. What started as an interview on conservation read more like lifestyles of the rich and shameless as Eleanor described how her household of seven plus ten servants saved food. "Making the ten servants help me do any saving has not only been possible, but highly profitable. Since I have started following the home-card instructions prices have risen, but my bills are no larger." The up-and-coming politician in FDR was horrified. He fired a letter back to his wife, "All I can say is that your latest newspaper campaign is a corker and I am proud to be the husband of the Originator, Discoverer and Inventor of the New Household Economy for Millionaires!" He went on, "Honestly, you have leaped into public fame, all Washington is talking of the Roosevelt Plan, and I begin to get telegrams of congratulations and requests for further details from Pittsburgh, New Orleans, San Francisco and other neighboring cities." A humiliated Eleanor wrote, "I feel dreadfully about it because so much is not true and yet some of it I did say. I will never be caught again that's sure and I'd like to crawl away for shame."

With Eleanor gone, Franklin and Lucy were free to enjoy each other's company. Just a week after Eleanor left town they were off again on the *Sylph* with Nigel Law and others in tow. FDR's light and breezy descriptions of the fun did little to allay his wife's suspicions. He meticulously names everyone on the trip to emphasize he's not alone with Lucy. He calls the group "a funny party, but it worked out splendidly." He further called the excursion "a bully trip." The group picnicked, swam, visited the Revolutionary War battlefield at Yorktown, lunched with an admiral on a battleship, and watched ships pass in review.

In August, an infected tonsil put Franklin in the hospital for four days. Eleanor returned from Campobello to care for her husband. Angry at his endless excuses for not joining her in their summer home, she felt ignored. "I don't think you read my letters for you never answer a question and nothing I ask for appears!" After two weeks she left but not without an ultimatum. He must come to Campobello. In a note to him on August 15 she says, "Remember I *count* on seeing you on the 26th. My threat is no idle one." According to Elliott Roosevelt, his mother was threatening to leave his father.

Lucy who once felt "part of the family" now sensed Eleanor's growing suspicions and responded. Struggles over trivial matters masked the real rivalry between the two women. Eleanor sent Lucy a check to pay for her work in the wool distribution and knitting projects for the war effort. Lucy returned the check, Eleanor sent it again, Lucy returned it yet again. Eleanor wrote Franklin of the situation on September 8, "I've written Miss Mercer and returned the check saying I knew she had done far more work than I could pay for. She is evidently quite cross with me!" Franklin replied on September 9 that Secretary of the Navy Josephus Daniels, in his quarrel with the Navy League, had disbanded the

Comforts Committee and was forming a rival knitting group under the Red Cross. Franklin had the last word, "*You* are entirely disconnected, and Lucy Mercer and Mrs. Munn are closing up the loose ends." Mrs. Charlie Munn was not only an old friend who worked closely with Eleanor and Lucy in their war work but also accompanied Lucy and Franklin on their outings.

Despite Eleanor's suspicions, FDR did not curtail his social events or reporting them to his wife. By August 19, he tells of taking Lucy and others on a car trip to visit friends near Harpers Ferry, Virginia. Dutifully he reports his activities to Eleanor, "Lucy Mercer went and the Graysons and we got there at 5:30 walked over the farm—a very rich one and left at nine and got home at midnight! The day was magnificent, but the road more dusty and even more crowded than when we went to Gettysburg."

By the fall of 1917 with Eleanor at Hyde Park until November, gossips talked of Lucy's affair with Roosevelt. Despite the wagging tongues, their courtship only intensified, for they were deeply in love. For Lucy he was "the love of her life." Emboldened by their affections, Roosevelt and Lucy met at friends' homes and dined in public.

Alice Roosevelt Longworth welcomed the couple. In the same manner as Lucy's mother, she loved being outrageous. She smoked in public, drove too fast, partied too long and loud. As president, her father Theodore had declared, "I can either run the country or I can control Alice. I cannot possibly do both." The press reported her exploits and dubbed her "Princess Alice." She inspired the color Alice blue and the song "Alice Blue Gown." She married playboy congressman Nicholas Longworth from Ohio in 1906 at the White House.* A range of personalities from politicians to bohemians passed through her salon, which boasted

*Longworth (1869–1931) served in Congress from 1903–1913 and 1915–1931. He was Speaker of the House from 1925–1931.

a couch decorated with an embroidered velvet cushion, "If you can't say something good about anyone, come and sit by me."

Alice and Eleanor shared flamboyant brothers who were distant fathers and contributed to difficult childhoods for both women. Alice lost her mother when she was two days old, was raised by Auntie Bye, and had a stormy relationship with her stepmother when her father remarried. When Alice left the White House after her marriage, her stepmother told her, "I want you to know that I'm glad to see you leave. You have never been anything but trouble." Yet, despite shared plights, Alice never approved of her cousin Eleanor's serious ways. "She always wanted to discuss things like whether contentment was better than happiness and whether they conflicted with one another," Alice complained. "Things like that, which I didn't give a damn about."

Alice's own marriage was in trouble, for she and husband Longworth seemed to be in a contest of bad behavior. He gambled and drank excessively, so much so that she later retorted, "He'd rather be tight than be President." He chased women. She liked to show her friends the window from which he'd jumped after an assignation with the Belgian ambassador's daughter. She became involved with the married senator William E. Borah whose moniker the "stallion of Idaho" leaves little to the imagination. Her longtime involvement with him earned her the nickname "Aurora Borah Alice."

Alice enjoyed encouraging Lucy and Franklin. She found Lucy "beautiful, charming, and an absolutely delightful creature." Alice recognized that Lucy and Franklin were "devoted to each other." She condoned the affair, "He *deserved* a good time. He was married to Eleanor."

Alice teased her cousin Franklin, "I saw you 20 miles out in the country. You didn't see me. Your hands were on the wheel but your eyes were on that perfectly lovely lady." "Isn't she perfectly lovely?" replied the besotted man. Motoring about the countryside gave Lucy and FDR the privacy they craved from their early days together to the day before FDR died.

Mrs. Edith Morton Eustis, daughter of Levi Morton, President Benjamin Harrison's vice president, was an old friend of Franklin and Lucy. She also entertained the lovers. Her home, Corcoran House, was conveniently located between the Navy Department and the Roosevelt house. They sometimes drove to her country home, Oatlands, outside Washington, D.C., in Virginia horse country. Even Auntie Bye's own son, W. Sheffield Cowles, Jr., years later reported that he had seen Franklin and Lucy out and about in Washington, "often, I used to think, too often."

Roosevelt loved this subterfuge. From his birth, he was a man surrounded by those who adored him. Having his very own secrets, secrets he felt would shock those who thought they knew him, gave him a measure of independence.

Lucy loved this older man because he was handsome, charming, and loved her. Like her absent father, he was unattainable, and soon Lucy would lose both of them.

CHAPTER 5

"Not willing to step aside"

Lucy and Franklin's warm summer of romance progressed to a chilly fall. Lucy's ailing father lived out his last days, and Eleanor returned to a Washington of wagging tongues about her husband and her former secretary.

On September 11, 1917, Carroll Mercer's lifestyle caught up with him, and he checked into Sibley Hospital. Dr. Norman R. Jenner declared Mercer ill with nephritis, a kidney inflammation caused by his Bright's disease, and valve disease of the heart. On Thursday the thirteenth he died from "cardiac decompensation" and exhaustion. He would have been sixty in December. The *Washington Post* obituary named him "one of the most widely known of the old residents of the District." *Town Topics* stated his funeral showed "some semblance of his former state, attended by old cronies who served as pall-bearers" and noted that Mrs. Mercer "did not appear at the funeral." For service to his country, Major Mercer was interred in Arlington National Cemetery. He made two wills, one from 1893 in which he left everything to Minnie and another from 1906 bestowing his property to his daughters. In reality, debts were his legacy. All his life Mercer had hoped to inherit money from his Aunt Sallie, the Countess Esterhazy, to support his expensive, gentlemanly pursuits. Ironically, the countess, aged seventy-two, died a month after her nephew. Minnie did get a thousand pounds from the countess's estate, but later filed in 1919 for a veteran's pension as Mercer's widow. Minnie always insisted that her estranged husband was "ill continuously until he died" and subsequently died "due to illness contracted in the Spanish American War."

Despite her parents' estrangement, Lucy had remained in contact with her father in his declining years. She wrote to him and visited him often. No matter the nature of their relationship, a father's death can mean a daughter's questioning of her own life's goals and values. At twenty-six, Lucy Page Mercer was not married in an era and social strata where young women were expected to be married by the age of twenty-one as Eleanor had. Lucy's own mother had been married twice by the age of twenty-five. Lucy was deeply in love with an older married man, the father of five between the ages of one and eleven, and she did not know the future of their liaison. She had forsaken any other suitors for him. If they were to be together, he would have to divorce Eleanor, and divorce carried an extreme social stigma. As Alice Roosevelt Longworth declared,

> I don't think one can have any idea how horrendous even the idea of divorce was in those days. I remember telling my family in 1912 that I wanted one and, although they didn't quite lock me up they exercised considerable pressure to get me to reconsider. Told me to think it over very carefully indeed. The whole thing would have caused too much of a hullabaloo apparently. In those days people just didn't go around divorcing one another. Not done, they said. Emphatically.

As much as Lucy loved and wanted Franklin, she was a devout Catholic with a faith that had sustained her through difficult times. Although her mother had divorced and remarried, the thought of marrying a divorced man troubled Lucy. Franklin did not need to convert to her faith, but his marriage to Eleanor would have to be annulled before Lucy could take the sacraments of her church. If they had children, they would raise them in the Catholic faith.

On October 5, 1917, after only serving four months and rising to yeoman third class, Lucy left the Navy Department "by Special Order of Secretary of the Navy." Her top rating qualified her for reenlistment. Once again, *Town Topics* linked Lucy to Nigel Law. The society sheet reported, "The gossip in Washington concerning a charming young girl" and "an equally delightful young man. . . . It would be an ideal match, as the young couple's ideas entirely harmonize. As the girl has recently gone into retirement because of family bereavement, the affair may reach a culmination sooner than expected." No need to mention names. Nigel Law left for England in December 1917 to find new staff for the Washington embassy. He could no longer be the designated escort for Lucy, not that anyone was fooled.

Washington whispered increasingly louder that Lucy and Franklin were in love. Eleanor heard of it in the one place that had been her refuge, her volunteer work. "There was a heavy blast of gossip and a lot came from the Patten sisters though Mary Patten worked at the R. R. Canteen and in E. R.'s group & E. R. was always fond of her and counted her in for particular occasions," wrote Mrs. Charles Sumner Hamlin, Washington maven and Roosevelt friend, in her diary. Word around Washington was that the three Patten sisters were such notorious scandal spreaders that the saying went, "Don't telegraph, don't telephone, tell-a-Patten." If Eleanor was aware of the gossips who worked with her at the canteen, cousin Alice's goading was worse. Eleanor related an encounter to Franklin visiting his mother at Hyde Park.

> This afternoon I went to the Capitol about 4. . . . On the way out I parted with Alice at the door not having allowed her to tell me any secrets. She inquired if you had told me and I said no and that I did not believe in knowing things which your husband did not wish you to know so I think I will be spared any further mysterious secrets!

When it comes to infidelity, "you are the last to know," goes the old saying, and Eleanor had stated, "I did not believe in knowing things which your husband did not wish you to know." Yet, the deceived partner always knows when a loved one is slipping away. For a while, it is just too painful to admit it.

That October three women, not only his beloved and his wife, but now his mother, grasped at FDR. In the midst of comforting Lucy over the loss of her father, he quarreled with his mother over his role in society. On a visit, Sara asked Franklin to promise to care for Hyde Park "that it will be kept in the family forever, just as my family has held on to Delano property." Sensing the tensions between her son and daughter-in-law, Sara stressed tradition over personal pleasure, the importance of home and family, and the responsibilities of those, such as her son, born with special privileges and talents—"noblesse oblige" and "honneur oblige." Sara had stressed to her son all of his life, "People of social position like ourselves should behave nobly toward others." Was her son behaving nobly? In her letter to both Eleanor and Franklin, after their weekend visit, she states,

> I thought: after all, would it not be better just to spend all one has at once in this time of suffering and need, and not think of the future . . . the old fashioned traditions of family life, simple home pleasures and refinements, and the traditions some of us love best, of what use is it to *keep up things*, to hold on to dignity and all I stood up for this evening. Do not say I *misunderstood*. I understood perfectly. But I cannot believe that my precious Franklin really feels as he expressed himself.

Franklin, torn by his love for Lucy, had argued for individual happiness over familial obligation. He was not willing to promise anything "forever" at this point. Sara's letter ends with the sentiment, "I may continue to feel that *home* is the best and happiest place and that my son and daughter and their children will live in peace and keep from tarnish which seems to affect so many. . . ." All knew what the impending tarnish was, but no one was willing to speak directly of it yet.

During this traumatic time, Eleanor turned to her mother-in-law, and the two women were probably as close as they ever were or would be. Sara's no nonsense, confidence eased Eleanor's lifelong fear of abandonment. "I shall never be able to hold him. He is so attractive," Eleanor had cried at her engagement to Franklin. Now she sensed her fears were coming true. To a woman who was often critical of her, Eleanor wrote, "Very few mothers I know mean as much to their daughters as you do to me." Eleanor knew that despite Sara's fondness of Lucy and her devotion to Franklin, her mother-in-law would support her when the time came to defend her marriage.

* * *

Activity can occupy the mind and keep personal problems at bay for a time. By 1918 the main characters in this love story were avoiding thinking of the confrontation each knew was inevitable.

Even if her parents had lived separate lives, Lucy's mother relied on her more than ever for both emotional and monetary support after Carroll Mercer's death. The fifty-four-year-old Minnie did not enjoy being a poor, fading beauty. Now at the Toronto Apartments in Washington, Lucy and Minnie entertained visiting maternal relatives, the Hendersons of North Carolina. As outrageous as Lucy's young cousins found her mother for smoking, they found Lucy "fine, and her smile was most beautiful and winning. . . ." Lucy found refuge by traveling to North Carolina just as her mother had when she divorced years earlier. "She was with me in Salisbury when the affair was at its height, but they realized it was hopeless," wrote Mrs. Elizabeth Henderson Cotten, Minnie's cousin, of Lucy and Franklin's affair.

Franklin Roosevelt wanted out of Washington. Sitting behind a desk during a war did not look good for a future political career. When he planned to volunteer for service in Europe, President Wilson informed his secretary of the navy, Josephus Daniels, to tell his assistant secretary, "that his only and best war service is to stay where he is." Roosevelt was not so easily deterred. With insistent lobbying and some luck, he obtained permission from Daniels to go to Europe on an inspection tour of navy facilities in the summer of 1918. Wilson allowed Roosevelt to leave because the president wanted Daniels to stay in Washington. After he sailed on July 9, FDR wrote Eleanor, "The more I think of it, the more I feel that being only thirty-six my place is not at a Washington desk, even a Navy desk."

Eleanor sent the children to their grandmother at Hyde Park that summer and threw herself into her war work. She kept her schedule so hectic, sometimes working sixteen hours a day, greeting the up to ten troop trains, carrying three to four thousand men a day, that came through Union Station. "Sometimes I wondered if I could live that way another day." She wrote Franklin on July 20 that the Red Cross had asked her to go to England to start a canteen there. Although she called it "a temptation," in her desire to get away, she declined, choosing to "stay with my children and do what work I could at home."

The purposefully filled lives of Lucy, Franklin, and Eleanor moved through 1918 until Franklin's illness forced each to confront the personal crisis that changed all their lives. On September 12, Eleanor was at Hyde Park when a telegram arrived from the Navy Department. Franklin had double pneumonia and the deadly influenza that killed so many at the end of World War I. Many men on his returning ship, the *Leviathan*, had already died and been buried at sea. Eleanor met his ship in New York with a doctor and an ambulance on September 19. She recalled years later in her autobiography, "My husband did not seem to me so seriously ill as the doctors implied." Yet, four orderlies bore him off the ship to the ambulance and carried him up the steps of his mother's house at East 65th Street. At some point Eleanor unpacked the bags of her ailing husband and found love letters from Lucy written while he was overseas. Elliott Roosevelt wrote in *An Untold Story: The Roosevelts of Hyde Park* that he believed his mother found the letters on September 20, 1918.

These letters validated Eleanor's worst fears. Twenty-five years later she wrote, "The bottom dropped out of my own particular world and I faced myself, my surroundings, my world, honestly for the first time."

Many biographers and historians have related the story of Eleanor finding the letters that proved Lucy and Franklin's love affair.* What followed that event is not so easy to surmise. Little commentary comes from the main participants as the letters and diaries of those involved during this crucial time have not survived or do not address the situation. The love letters from Lucy to Franklin, sadly but understandably, were probably destroyed after Eleanor found them, read them, and confronted her husband with them. If Lucy had a diary or discussed FDR with friends or relatives via letters, they haven't surfaced. Sara Roosevelt kept detailed diaries all of her life but does not mention

*Olive Clapper's 1946 book, *Washington Tapestry*, is the earliest published account of the love affair although she does not mention Lucy by name. "Mrs. Roosevelt was supposed to have called her husband and the enamored woman to a conference, at which she offered to give her husband a divorce if the woman wished to marry him. A Catholic, the woman could not marry a divorced man" (p. 238).

this family crisis. There is no written record by Franklin concerning this period of his life with Lucy. Eleanor later wrote cryptically of this difficult time and discussed it only with her closest friends.

Details must be deduced from the comments of others, and naturally, they differ from the Lucy camp to the Roosevelt camp. Anyone who has ever been in love and felt betrayed, or in love and the secret revealed, or in love and torn between two can imagine the words that passed among those involved.

Lucy and Franklin wanted to marry but couldn't because, "Eleanor was not willing to step aside," Lucy told her cousin Elizabeth Cotten. According to Cotten, Lucy felt the religious difficulties between the two "could have been arranged" through an annulment. Lucy, as spirited as her mother and father, had lived a life of emotional highs and lows. She had witnessed her parents' relationship. She knew what grand passion was, for she had loved Roosevelt for four years. She knew the consequences of loving a married man, yet she chose to be with him. She also chose to give him up for his own good, but she would never stop loving him. "It was a real love for each other and . . . it lasted through the years," Cotten recalled. A measure of Lucy's love for Franklin can be seen in her discretion about him her entire life.

Divorce was an option, and Eleanor seriously thought about it. Elliott Roosevelt believed his mother "preferred a divorce. That was her first thought, and her first tactic was to offer it. She had grounds in the state of New York, which recognized only adultery. The letters were her proof." James Roosevelt wrote of a "well-kept-secret" which was also evidence—a motel register from Virginia Beach showing Lucy and FDR had checked in as a married couple. In 1918 a journey by car from Washington to Virginia Beach in a day, then spending the night and driving back to Washington the next day tests the imagination. The only road was long and meandering. There were few if any gas stations in 1918. A jaunt of 250 miles would have been quite an undertaking. Would Roosevelt as undersecretary of the navy have registered under his own name?

Anna wrote that her mother informed her of Lucy and her father when she was seventeen in 1923. She recalled that her mother "offered him a divorce and asked that he take time to think things over carefully before giving her a definite answer." Eleanor also told her daughter that her father "voluntarily promised" to end the "romantic relationship."

"Always remember, Alice, that Eleanor offered Franklin his freedom," Auntie Corinne, Theodore Roosevelt's youngest sister, told Alice Longworth.* Alice's version of the situation was "Apparently there was a family conclave, presided over by Cousin Sally, and they talked over the whole matter of a divorce and they decided that there was Franklin with five children and Lucy, a Catholic, and they had better call it off."**

How far Lucy and Franklin and Eleanor had progressed in their plans as to divorce and marriage may never be known, but it was such that they decided to "call it off." The person most responsible for that decision was Alice's Cousin Sally or Sara, Franklin's mother. She held her most persuasive argument in her purse. "Mama" paid her son's household expenses, paid for the

*Eleanor told friends in later years that when she confronted Franklin she offered him a divorce if "after considering its impact upon the children that was what he wanted" (Ward, p. 413).

**The columnist Drew Pearson wrote in 1968 that Eleanor and Franklin met at a friend's New York apartment, Elsie Cobb Wilson, who had once employed Lucy, to discuss their divorce. According to Mrs. Wilson, Eleanor refused to divorce him because it would end his political career. Another version of this story has Mrs. Wilson persuading Lucy to end the romance. Pearson also wrote that while driving through Virginia in the summer of 1917, Eleanor had seen her husband embracing Lucy in a parked car and confronted him afterwards. Eleanor did not learn to drive until the summer of 1918.

children's education, paid for family trips, and countless other things until she died in 1941. When Franklin and Eleanor married, their combined income a year from each of their father's estates was around $12,500.* It was a comfortable sum for 1905, but Sara wanted her son and his family to live as well as he had under her roof. Both Franklin and Eleanor allowed her to provide that lifestyle. At a family meeting Sara declared, "It was all very well for you, Eleanor, to speak of being 'willing to give Franklin his freedom.'" As far as Sara was concerned if her son disgraced her family with a divorce, she would "not give him another dollar," nor would he inherit the beloved family home, Springwood at Hyde Park.

Lucy's Catholicism would also have troubled the Episcopalian Sara. She and others in her class saw the Roman Catholic religion as two distinct groups. The first was the Catholicism of the early Maryland founders to which Lucy's family belonged, but Franklin's mother would also identify it as the superstitious faith of the multitudes of Irish and Italian immigrants in the United States who largely held menial jobs.

If FDR had divorced Eleanor, he would have lost his job as assistant secretary of the navy. His boss Josephus Daniels, a fundamentalist Christian, had no patience for low moral standards. As Secretary of the Navy, he banned alcohol from the officers' mess. He stopped issuing condoms for sailors on shore leave. He favored virginity and abstinence for both sexes prior to marriage. He favored fidelity in marriage. When his brother-in-law wanted a divorce, Daniels fired him from the family newspaper in North Carolina.

Then there was the matter of Roosevelt's political career. Louis Howe, the former Albany newspaperman turned political adviser who worked for FDR until his death in 1936, knew divorce would

*By today's standards that would be over $100,000.

end Roosevelt's political career. Losing family, money, ancestral home, and a political career tipped the scale against divorce and remarriage to Lucy. Elliott recalled,

> It wasn't just Sara, it was Louis Howe going back and forth and just reasoning, convincing father that he had no political future if he did this. Lucy would not marry a divorced man, she was an ardent Catholic. Louis did a selling job. Father wanted to give it up and mother felt betrayed and had a primitive outlook on it, but she came around because Louis convinced her. He said she could not destroy Franklin's goal and he convinced her that she too would have a great role to play. He convinced her it was better for the children.

Eleanor believed it was Howe's influence more than any other person who persuaded FDR to give up a life with Lucy. No matter how those involved made the final decision, Eleanor insisted that Franklin and Lucy never see each other again.

Franklin and Eleanor would stay together. When Eleanor's children approached her in later years on the subject of their divorces, she encouraged them. Among the five Roosevelt children, they had twenty-one marriages.

James recalled that his parents

> . . . agreed to go on for the sake of appearances, the children and the future, but as business partners, not as husband and wife, provided he end his affair with Lucy at once, which he did. After that Father and Mother had an armed truce that endured to the day he died, despite several occasions I was to observe in which he in one way or another held out his arms to mother and she flatly refused to enter his embrace.

The transformation from Eleanor Roosevelt, dutiful wife and mother to Eleanor Roosevelt, independent woman and activist, was underway.

Eleanor's cousin Corrine Robinson Alsop described the outcome of the family crisis, "Everybody behaved well and exactly as one would expect each of the protagonists to behave." Although the affair seemed to be over, it changed those involved forever. Mrs. Alsop felt Franklin's love for Lucy "seemed to release something in him. Up to the time that Lucy Mercer came into Franklin's life he seemed to look at human relationships cooly, calmly, and without depth. He viewed his family dispassionately, and enjoyed them, but he had in my opinion a loveless quality, as if he were incapable of emotion." Her husband, Joe Alsop, observed, "He emerged tougher and more resilient, wiser and more profound even before his struggle with polio."

Eleanor felt deceived by not only her husband, but also a woman she had regarded warmly, and her friends and family who had known of and encouraged the affair. The betrayal would scar her for life. "I have the memory of an elephant. I can forgive, but I cannot forget," she said years later.

When she died in 1962 a newspaper clipping of a poem, Virginia Moore's "Psyche," lay at her bedside. Eleanor had written "1918" at the top of the clipping.

The soul that has believed
And is deceived
Thinks nothing for a while
All thoughts are vile.
And then because the sun
Is mute persuasion,
And hope in Spring and Fall
Most natural,
The soul grows calm and mild
A little child,
Finding the pull of breath
Better than death . . .
The soul that had believed
And was deceived
Ends by believing more
Than ever before.

World War I, "the war to end all wars" as some called it, ended November 11, 1918, with nearly forty million casualties. The worldwide flu epidemic following in its wake claimed possibly another thirty million. A nation mourned the passing of Theodore Roosevelt on January 6, 1919.

Millions are difficult to comprehend; yet individuals know what grief and mourning are. Lucy had lost a father and then a lover in just a little over a year. She had lost a woman she considered a friend. She had tested her faith. Then twenty-seven, she had her whole life ahead of her, and it looked as if it would be that of a poor spinster. She daily witnessed what had become of her mother, and that is not what she wanted. As Lucy had done in the past, she retreated to Salisbury, North Carolina, to reassemble the pieces of her broken heart. Soon she would meet a man who would determine her future, Winthrop Rutherfurd.

CHAPTER 6

"Like an English peer"

In comparison to Lucy's and Roosevelt's forebears, the Rutherfurds were newcomers. Winthrop's paternal ancestor Walter Rutherfurd, the son of Sir John Rutherfurd, left his Scottish homeland in 1756 to fight in the French and Indian War, which had begun two years earlier. Walter was a career army soldier who came from a long line of Celtic warriors.* The Rutherfurds had lived on the border of Scotland and England and fought with both William Wallace and Robert the Bruce against the English. Now in the New World, Walter Rutherfurd fought to secure British control of North America east of the Mississippi. Like many who came to this country with the intention of returning home, he decided to stay. Although the war did not end until 1763, Major Rutherfurd with twenty years of military service retired to New York City in 1760 with his wife Catherine Parker.

*"Ruther" is Celtic for red. The "furd" may come from a story that the clan beat back invaders at a stream.

While Walter was sympathetic to American patriots in their war against the British, he wanted to stay out of the conflict. He moved his family to his summer home in Hunterdon County in New Jersey to wait out the war. In 1777, patriots held him as a loyalist hostage to ensure the safety of American soldiers being held by the British. He remained under guard in Morristown, New Jersey, until the end of the war in 1781. He then returned home to New York City and died there in 1804.

The Morris family had been in America since the Restoration in England in 1660. They gave their name to many pieces of real estate including Morristown, New Jersey, and Morrisania, New York, where Lewis Morris Rutherfurd was born. Both Winthrop's grandfather, Robert, and his great-grandfather, John, married Morrises. Lewis Morris Rutherfurd was named for Lewis Morris, the first governor of New Jersey in 1738.

It was Walter's son John Rutherfurd (1760–1840) who settled in Allamuchy, New Jersey in 1787 to buy the land that eventually became the Rutherfurd estate. He served as a New Jersey senator in Congress from 1791–1798. His son, Robert Rutherfurd, became the father of the famous astronomer Lewis (1816–1892).

As his grandfather and father, Lewis Morris Rutherfurd entered the legal profession, the favored profession of generations of Rutherfurds. He worked his way into a partnership with William H. Seward who later became Lincoln's secretary of state.* Gazing at the heavens was Rutherfurd's first love for he had studied science at Williams College in Massachusetts. After twelve years practicing law, he left in 1849 to become an astronomer. With his own money and what he called "years of struggle," he built an observatory in Manhattan in 1856. A

*Seward continued as secretary of state under President Andrew Johnson. He supported the purchase of Alaska from Russia for seven million dollars. Detractors called it "Seward's folly."

pioneer in spectral analysis using the new technology of photography, he photographed the moon, sun, Saturn, and Jupiter with a telescope specially fitted to a camera, an invention he called the spectroscope. He used his photos of the universe to map star clusters, and he measured the distance between stars in his images with another of his inventions, the micrometer. Astronomers today still use his methods, only with more powerful telescopes and cameras.

As distinguished as Winthrop Rutherfurd's ancestry was on his father's side, that of his mother, Margaret Stuyvesant, was not only illustrious but brought with it a fortune. The name Stuyvesant is associated with New York history and legend, and she was a direct descendant of Peter Stuyvesant born in Holland in 1592. He came to New Netherlands in 1647 after he had already served as a colonial governor of Curacoa in the West Indies. He was a true "Knickerbocker" named for the knee-length trousers worn by the early Dutch settlers. By the nineteenth century the term *Knickerbockers* referred to the moneyed, social elite of New York City who traced their ancestry back to this era.

Whether Peter Minuet of the Dutch West India Company purchased Manhattan from the Lenape Indians for twenty-four dollars worth of trinkets is true or not, it was Stuyvesant who acquired much property in what would become Manhattan. Washington Irving in his *Knickerbocker's History of New York* described him as "A tough, sturdy, valiant, weather-beaten, mettlesome, obstinate, leathern-sided, lion-hearted, generous-spirited old governor." Stuyvesant served as governor of New Netherlands until 1664 when the English took over the Dutch colony, and it became New York and New Amsterdam became New York City.

Winthrop's mother also pointed to John Winthrop, and thus her son's name, on her family tree. John Winthrop, the first governor of the Massachusetts Bay Colony, settled in America ten years after the Pilgrims landed at Plymouth. He was a shrewd administrator who negotiated a charter, making his settlement a self-governing colony free from interference of the mother country. This meant the people of the colony were free to make their own laws, establish schools, levy taxes, and other societal transactions as they saw fit. Winthrop served as governor 1629–1634 and from 1638 until his death in 1649.

Into this world of ancestry and affluence, Winthrop Rutherfurd was born in 1862 in his father's mansion in one of the most fashionable sections of the New York City, Tenth Street and Second Avenue. Rutherfurd grew up leading the life that Carroll Mercer desired—gentleman and sportsman. The *Telegram* described Winthrop's childhood adventures in 1900, "While he [Lewis Morris Rutherfurd] peered through a great telescope and conned the dog stars, his boys used to get up dog fights in the stable yard back of the house." An early interest in dogs lead Winthrop to become one of the top breeders of fox terriers in the country.

He belonged to all the right clubs, Westminster Kennel, Knickerbocker, New York Yacht, Racquet and Tennis. He studied law and graduated from Columbia College, later University, in 1884. He even rode to the hounds with Theodore Roosevelt, as did Eleanor Roosevelt's father, Elliott Roosevelt. Theodore Roosevelt wrote his friend Henry Cabot Lodge in 1886 of their hunting exploits. "Poor old Elliott broke his collar bone the third time he was out with the hounds; so did Winty Rutherfurd."

If wealth and social status weren't enough to make him New York's most eligible bachelor, "breathtaking good looks" completed the package. He even had a hint of scandal about him. Rumors circulated that he had been involved with Ava Lowle Willing Astor, wife of Colonel John Jacob Astor and daughter-in-law of society maven "the" Mrs. Astor. The couple did divorce in 1910. Astor perished on the *Titanic* in 1912. Ava eventually became Lady Ribblesdale when she married Thomas Lister, Fourth Baron Ribblesdale in 1919.

Edith Wharton, the novelist of New York society, grew up knowing the Rutherfurds. She called Winty "the prototype of my first novels."

As a young man, Winty played a role in a societal drama worthy of both Wharton and Henry James, although his part wasn't publicly known until 1926. It all started when his friend William K. Vanderbilt invited him for a cruise on his yacht, the world's largest, *The Valiant*. Alva and William K. Vanderbilt planned the excursion to shore up their faltering marriage. William K. was the grandson of Cornelius Vanderbilt and the son of William Henry Vanderbilt, both considered the richest men in America during their lifetimes. It was William K.'s brother Frederick William Vanderbilt who bought an estate near the Roosevelts' Springwood in Hyde Park in 1895.

William K. had married Alva Smith in 1875. Alva was born in Mobile, Alabama, the daughter of a salesman, but a man of land, who liked to claim that his family descended from an extinct line of nobility, the Earls of Stirling in Scotland. Whether true or not, it was enough for even Alva to look down her nose at Vanderbilts who had made their money in the commerce of railroads and ships. After the Civil War, her family settled in New York. An intelligent and well-educated woman, she had studied in France. What she lacked in fashionable beauty, for her detractors said she looked like a frog, she made up in ambition. She boasted, "I always do everything first. I blaze the trail for the rest to walk in. I was the first girl of my set to marry a Vanderbilt." Being first was the mission statement of Alva's life.

She set out with her fortitude and her husband's fortune to be queen of New York society. All of New York society "eagerly sought" an invitation to Alva's costume ball given on March 26, 1883 to open her new house at 660 Fifth Avenue built by Richard

Morris Hunt, who had also built the Rutherfurd home at 175 South Avenue. Alva invited twelve hundred excluding Mrs. Caroline Astor, the wife of William Backhouse Astor, Jr., the grandson of John Jacob Astor who had made his fortune in fur trading and real estate. She was the gatekeeper of the inner sanctum of New York's elite. If Mrs. Astor didn't "know" you, you weren't known, and Mrs. Astor didn't want to know the Vanderbilts. As part of old Knickerbocker New York society, she considered them to have too much money and too little class. The Vanderbilts had not been invited to Mrs. Astor's annual ball to celebrate the chosen Four Hundred of New York's elite, and Alva hadn't forgiven, let alone forgotten. The Rutherfurds had been included. As the social superior, Mrs. Astor must make the first move, and she hadn't called on Alva, the newcomer. Now Mrs. Astor's daughter, Carrie, wanted to attend the ball, as she and her friends had been practicing a special quadrille dance. It was social blackmail, but the loving mother knew what she had to do or there would be no invitation. Mrs. Astor received her party invitation only after her footman dressed in a blue uniform copied from Windsor Castle left her calling card engraved "Mrs. Astor" in Alva's silver tray held by her liveried footman dressed in maroon in the foyer of her new Fifth Avenue home. The Vanderbilts were crass outsiders no more. The *New York World* chronicled the high cost of rising to the top of New York society. The expense of costumes, flowers, carriages, catering, music, and champagne totaled over $250,000.* A magazine later stated, "The Vanderbilts have come nobly forward to show the world how millionaires should live."

William K. and Alva produced three children, Consuelo born in 1877, William K. II in 1878, and Harold Stirling in 1883. Alva's "fourth child" was one of the most famous "summer" homes of the palatial Newport area called Marble House, constructed

*The equivalent today would be about $7.5 million for the party.

between 1889 and 1892. Wealth, social status, grand houses, or family could not hold the marriage together. Consuelo Vanderbilt in her memoir *The Glitter and the Gold* remarked, "Why my parents ever married remains a mystery to me."

> My father had a generous and unselfish nature; his pleasure was to see people happy and he enjoyed the company of his children and friends, but my mother—for reasons I can but ascribe to a towering ambition—opposed these carefree views with all the force of her strong personality.

A long cruise might curtail the rumors about the disintegrating eighteen-year marriage. Consuelo remembered, "It was in such an atmosphere of dread and uncertainty that our last and longest yachting expedition was undertaken in my seventeenth year." On board *The Valiant* were Alva and William K., daughter Consuelo, and younger son Harold. In addition, William K. brought some of his sporting friends, all rich, all horse lovers; they even all used the same architect, Hunt. Oliver Hazard Perry Belmont was the thirty-five-year-old son of the international banker, August Belmont.* Then there was thirty-one-year-old Winthrop Rutherfurd. Also on board was a crew of seventy-two plus a French chef, a doctor, and a governess.

The cruise left New York on November 23, 1893, to sail the Mediterranean, through the Suez Canal into the Red Sea and Indian Ocean. From Bombay, they left their yacht to cross India by train. The Vanderbilts were used to luxury travel on their railway lines. Here they learned, according to Consuelo, "what discomfort in a train could amount to. At every station angry natives seeking transportation tried noisily to force their way into our bedrooms. . . ." At the port of Hooghly they reunited with *The Valiant* and their chef, who was most welcome, after the travelers

*The Belmont Stakes, the third leg of the triple crown of horseracing, is named for August Belmont, the first president of the American Jockey Club.

had lived on "tea, toast and marmalade" because the "food was incredibly nasty" in Consuelo's words.

The physical journey resulted in much internal change for the Vanderbilt family. William K. and Alva's marriage ended; Alva decided Consuelo's future; and Consuelo fell in love with Winthrop Rutherfurd. By Bombay, Alva and her husband were no longer speaking. They traveled on separately to reach Paris in the spring of 1894. Alva heard that her husband had not only set up a household for "a woman notorious in Europe" but when she found out that the woman's servants were dressed in the same maroon uniforms as her servants, it was the last nail in the marriage's coffin. Cornelius, now the family patriarch and William K.'s older brother, came from New York to try to talk them out of the potential scandal of divorce. The woman who wanted to be first in everything wasn't afraid of tittle-tattle.

> I was the first woman of any prominence to sue for a divorce for adultery, and Society was by turns stunned, horrified, and then savage in its opposition and criticism. For a woman of my social standing to apply for a divorce from one of the richest men in the United States on such grounds, or for any cause, was an unheard of and glaring defiance of custom. It was a shock to everyone.

Alva was far too busy planning Consuelo's coming out party in Paris to worry about shocking anyone. At eighteen, Consuelo was considered the loveliest of the Vanderbilt women. She was tall, slender, intelligent, known as *"la belle Mlle. Vanderbilt au long cou"* because of her swanlike neck. In Paris five suitors asked Alva for Consuelo, but Alva considered "none of them sufficiently exalted."

Alva had already made up her mind. Her daughter would marry a peer of the realm, an English duke. Not just any duke but Charles Richard John Spencer Churchill, ninth duke of Marlborough, marquess of Blandford, earl of Sunderland, earl of

Marlborough, Baron Spencer of Wormleighton, Baron Churchill of Sandridge, prince of the Holy Roman Empire. While visiting Viceroy and Lady Lansdowne in India, Alva had settled on the duke, Lady Lansdowne's nephew, for Consuelo.

Known as "Sunny" for being earl of Sunderland, the duke didn't live up to his nickname. "Nothing on looks," declared Gertrude Vanderbilt, Consuelo's cousin. Shorter than Consuelo, he was critical, moody, no intellectual, but he was an available twenty-three-year-old duke, and he needed money. Blenheim Palace, situated on three thousand acres of Oxfordshire, needed someone with a Midas touch to maintain it.* The first duke of Marlborough, John Churchill, received Blenheim Palace from Queen Anne and a grateful British nation. He had defeated the French in 1704 near the Bavarian town of Blenheim during the War of the Spanish Succession. Modeled on Versailles, it took seventeen years to build. Preceding generations of Spencer-Churchills piled up debt. Even Sunny's father, the previous Duke of Marlborough, had married a widowed American heiress, Lily Hammersley, to infuse some funds into his bank account. Her money re-roofed the seven-acre palace, but it wasn't enough. Sunny was selling portions of the extensive Blenheim art collection just to live day to day. Only the Marlborough social position kept him afloat.

Consuelo was apprehensive about her parents' divorce. "I felt relief that the sinister gloom of their relationship would no longer encompass me. But I did not realise how irrevocably I would be cut off from a father I loved nor how completely my mother would dominate me from then on." Alva was well aware that Consuelo had fallen "violently in love" with Winthrop Rutherfurd

*Winston Churchill was born at Blenheim Palace in 1874. His father was Randolph Churchill, brother of the eighth duke; his mother was the American heiress, Jenny Jerome. Churchill and Sunny were cousins.

when they returned to New York for the winter season of 1894. Consuelo thought Marlborough was not interested in her. She had met him once at a dinner party in London, and he had barely spoken to her. Innocently she planned on studying languages and marrying Rutherfurd, for she felt her mother had given up her idea of her daughter marrying a duke. Not true, with her divorce behind her, Alva could turn her full attention to becoming the mother of a duchess.

Rutherfurd had won Consuelo's heart with "his outstanding looks, his distinction and his charm. . . ." Years later Lucy agreed with her artist and friend, Elizabeth Shoumatoff, when she remarked that Winthrop Rutherfurd "looked like an English peer with his chiseled features, sharp eyes, and a sarcastic expression around his mouth." On Consuelo's eighteenth birthday, he sent her "one perfect rose."* Later that day they went bicycle riding where she received "the only proposal of marriage I wished to accept." It had to be a secret engagement as Alva on her bicycle was fast closing on them. Winthrop promised to follow his secret fiancé as she was leaving for Europe the next day. Consuelo heard nothing from her Winty for five months. Unbeknownst to her, he had followed her to Paris. Alva confiscated his letters before Consuelo could see them and her daughter's letters before she could send them. She informed servants that Rutherfurd was to be "refused admittance when he called."

Alva relentlessly chaperoned her daughter making sure she was in Marlborough's presence as much as possible. Even a weekend visit to Blenheim did not tempt Consuelo. "I dreamed of life in my own country with my Rosenkavalier." Even though her mother had invited the duke to Newport in September, Consuelo planned her elopement. On her return to the United States,

*In Consuelo Vanderbilt's autobiography published in 1953 she never mentions Winthrop Rutherfurd by name but calls him "Rosenkavalier" or "Mr. X."

Consuelo found she was "a prisoner, with my mother and my governess as wardens" who never let her out of their sight. She did manage a brief dance with Winty at a ball before Alva tore her away. A battle of wills ensued between Consuelo and her mother.

> I suffered every searing reproach, heard every possible invective hurled at the man I loved. I was informed of his numerous flirtations, of his well-known love for a married woman, of his desire to marry an heiress. My mother even declared that he would have no children and that there was madness in his family.

Alva's final volley to Consuelo's resistance was that "she would not hesitate to shoot a man whom she considered would ruin my life." Cutoff from her lover, her father, fearing she caused her mother a heart attack, as Alva had taken to her bed, and fearing that her mother would kill Rutherfurd, "In utter misery I asked Mrs. Jay [her mother's friend] to let X know that I could not marry him."

On November 6, 1895, Alva got her duke; Marlborough got his money. Alva was so fearful that Consuelo would run off with Rutherfurd on her wedding day she placed a guard at Consuelo's bedroom door. Sunny received $2.5 million in Vanderbilt stock, an equivalent of $75 million today. The stock accumulated 4 percent a year, equivalent to three million dollars yearly today. The Vanderbilt fortune would cover any expenses of Consuelo, which included a town house in New York and more repairs to Blenheim.

The Rutherfurd-Vanderbilt saga did not end here. In 1903, Alva's ex-husband William K. married Anne Harriman Sands Rutherfurd, widow of Winthrop Rutherfurd's brother. Alva furiously banned the new Mrs. Vanderbilt from all society functions, but she could hardly cast stones for she had married her ex-husband's friend O. H. P. Belmont who had been on the infamous cruise.

Consuelo's marriage to Sunny was predictably unhappy, so after eleven years and producing the obligatory two sons, the heir and spare to the Marlborough titles, they separated in 1906 and divorced in 1920. Despite the iron hand Alva had used on her daughter to marry, she supported Consuelo's decision, "My mother came from America to be with me; her sympathy was precious. . . ."

By 1926, Marlborough had joined the Roman Catholic Church and wished to have his first marriage annulled in order to validate a second civil marriage. He asked for Consuelo's help. She had also remarried. Her second husband was Jacques Balsan, a French Catholic. In her words, all this "determined my decision to approach the Rota." Her claim to the annulment of her marriage to Marlborough was "I had been married against my will." On November 24, 1926, an announcement came from Rome that the Vatican Ecclesiastical Court, the Rota, annulled the marriage of the Duke of Marlborough and Consuelo Vanderbilt because Consuelo had been in love with "an American named Rutherfurd," but she had been forced by her mother to marry the Duke. In characteristic retiring fashion, Winthrop Rutherfurd replied simply to questions on his role in the affair, "Yes, some thirty years ago I knew Miss Vanderbilt and I was one of her great admirers."

Former Duchess of Marlborough, Consuelo Vanderbilt Balsan died on December 6, 1965. Among her personal treasures was a photograph of Winthrop Rutherfurd that she had kept all her years.

Figure 1: Franklin on his pony, his father and mother on the south lawn of Springwood at Hyde Park, New York around 1891 when Lucy was born. Courtesy of the Franklin D. Roosevelt Presidential Library.

Figure 2: Franklin at the age of seventeen with his father, James Roosevelt, twenty-six years senior to his mother Sara Delano. Courtesy of the Franklin D. Roosevelt Presidential Library.

Figure 3: Eleanor and Franklin Roosevelt shown shortly after their marriage in 1905. Courtesy of the Franklin D. Roosevelt Presidential Library.

Figure 4: Lucy Mercer about the time she came to work as Eleanor's social secretary in 1914. Courtesy of the Franklin D. Roosevelt Presidential Library.

Figure 5: Roosevelt as assistant secretary of the navy with Josephus Daniels, secretary of the navy. FDR captioned this photograph: "My chief and myself in the act of casting longing glances at the White House." Courtesy of the Franklin D. Roosevelt Presidential Library.

Figure 6: Alice Roosevelt Longworth, the daughter of Theodore Roosevelt, encouraged FDR's and Lucy's romance. Courtesy of the Franklin D. Roosevelt Presidential Library.

Figure 7: A family portrait, June 1919, after Eleanor offered her husband a divorce and his mother refused it. Front row seated: Anna, Franklin, Sara, Eleanor. Standing: Elliott, FDR, Jr., James, and John. Courtesy of the Franklin D. Roosevelt Presidential Library.

Figure 8: FDR and Eleanor at Campobello around 1920. He was stricken with polio in 1921. Courtesy of the Franklin D. Roosevelt Presidential Library.

Figure 9: Despite years of therapy, Roosevelt never stood or walked without heavy leg braces and others to support him. Here he stands with the aid of his son James during the 1932 presidential election. Courtesy of the Franklin D. Roosevelt Presidential Library.

Figure 10: Although Lucy married Winthrop Rutherfurd in 1920, she stayed in touch with Roosevelt over the years. This photograph was taken around the time of his first presidential election in 1932. Courtesy of Corbis.

Figure 11: Lucy attended FDR's first inauguration in March 1933 and all later ones at his invitation. Courtesy of the Franklin D. Roosevelt Presidential Library.

Figure 12: Franklin and Eleanor in the White House following his first inauguration. Courtesy of the Franklin D. Roosevelt Presidential Library.

Figure 13: Roosevelt with his three secretaries: Grace Tully, Stephen Early, Marguerite "Missy" LeHand. Courtesy of the Franklin D. Roosevelt Presidential Library.

Figure 14: Lorena Hickok and Earl Miller, July 1933. Both adored Eleanor and helped her overcome her fears of White House life. Courtesy of the Franklin D. Roosevelt Presidential Library.

Figure 15: Lucy as portrayed by the artist Elizabeth Shoumatoff. They became friends in 1937. Courtesy of the Franklin D. Roosevelt Presidential Library.

Figure 16: FDR shown working in front of the Little White House in Warm Springs, Georgia, as photographed by Margaret Suckley. Courtesy of the Franklin D. Roosevelt Presidential Library.

Figure 17: Missy LeHand in her third floor apartment at the White House. She was Roosevelt's secretary, confidante, and hostess from 1921 until her stroke in 1941. Courtesy of the Franklin D. Roosevelt Presidential Library.

Figure 18: Lucy, on the right, and Shoumatoff at Allamuchy, New Jersey around 1938. Shoumatoff wrote on the back of this photograph, "Painting the background for Mr. R's portrait with pups." Courtesy of the Franklin D. Roosevelt Presidential Library.

Figure 19: The Roosevelts with Crown Princess Martha of Norway who sought asylum in the United States in August 1940. Courtesy of the Franklin D. Roosevelt Presidential Library.

Figure 20: Sara Delano Roosevelt in her library at Hyde Park in 1941 just before her death. Courtesy of the Franklin D. Roosevelt Presidential Library.

Figure 21: Lucy, on the left, with Shoumatoff at Aiken, South Carolina. Courtesy of the Franklin D. Roosevelt Presidential Library.

Figure 22: FDR holding Fala with Ruthie Bie, February 1941 at Hilltop Cottage, Hyde Park, the home he designed to accommodate his paralysis. This is a rare photo taken by Margaret Suckley showing the president in his wheelchair. Courtesy of the Franklin D. Roosevelt Presidential Library.

Figure 23: Roosevelt on his train the *Ferdinand Magellan* with his cousins Margaret "Daisy" Suckley (left) and Laura "Polly" Delano. Major Henry Hooker of Fort Riley, Kansas is in the background, April 25, 1943. Courtesy of the Franklin D. Roosevelt Presidential Library.

Figure 24: FDR with his daughter, Anna Boettiger, greets the French General Charles de Gaulle, July 6, 1944. Secretary of State Cordell Hull is on the left. Courtesy of the Franklin D. Roosevelt Presidential Library.

Figure 25: The last inauguration of Franklin Roosevelt. Because of the war, the ceremony was held to a minimum. Vice President Harry Truman is on the far left. James Roosevelt salutes behind his father. Courtesy of the Franklin D. Roosevelt Presidential Library.

Figure 26: Eleanor and Franklin with their thirteen grandchildren taken immediately after the inauguration, January 20, 1945. Courtesy of the Franklin D. Roosevelt Presidential Library.

Figure 27: The Little White House at Warm Springs where Lucy visited Roosevelt. Courtesy of the Franklin D. Roosevelt Presidential Library.

Figure 28: Lucy by Nicholas Robbins, Elizabeth Shoumatoff's photographer. It was taken at Warm Springs the day before FDR died. Courtesy of the Franklin D. Roosevelt Presidential Library.

Figure 29: Robbins also photographed Roosevelt. At sixty-three, twelve years as president and the strains of World War II show on his face. He died the next day, April 12, 1945. Courtesy of the Franklin D. Roosevelt Presidential Library.

Figure 30: The horse drawn caisson carries the president's body past mourning crowds in Washington, D.C., April 14, 1945. Courtesy of the Franklin D. Roosevelt Presidential Library.

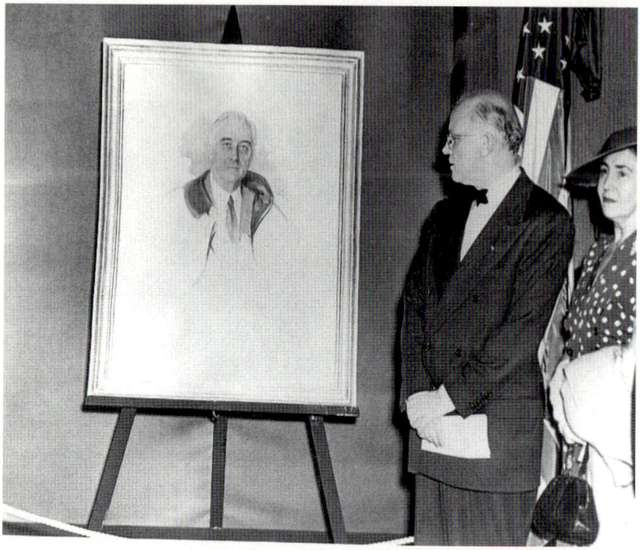

Figure 31: Shoumatoff unveiling the unfinished portrait of FDR she was working on when he suffered a stroke. Courtesy of the Franklin D. Roosevelt Presidential Library.

Figure 32: Lucy with her grandchildren. Lucy would lose her mother and her sister in 1947. In 1948 she was diagnosed with leukemia and died on July 31. Private Collection.

CHAPTER 7

"Please tell Franklin"

"It is a truth universally acknowledged that a single man in possession of a good fortune must be in want of a wife," begins *Pride and Prejudice* by Jane Austen, the nineteenth-century English oracle on society and marriage. Winthrop Rutherfurd was just such a man. He had lost his wife of fifteen years, Alice Morton, in June 1917, and he possessed a good fortune.

Alice was one of the five striking daughters of former Vice President Levi Morton. Morton had served as vice president from 1889 until 1893 under President Benjamin Harrison. In a quirk of fate, Morton might have been president if he had accepted James Garfield's offer to join his presidential ticket in 1880. Morton, a wealthy banker, refused the position because he preferred the post of secretary of the treasury. Charles J. Guiteau, a disgruntled office seeker, shot Garfield in 1881, and Vice President Chester A. Arthur became president. Morton did not become secretary of the treasury, as Garfield did not complete his cabinet before he died. The Republican Party again considered Morton as a candidate for president in 1896, but McKinley won the top spot with Theodore Roosevelt as his vice president. When the deranged anarchist Leon Czolgosz shot McKinley and Theodore Roosevelt became president in 1901, Morton must have considered how figuratively dodging assassins' bullets had affected his life.

Despite that he was never president by nomination, election, or assassination, he led a distinguished life of public service in addition to the vice presidency. Voters elected him to Congress in 1878 and 1880. He became the United States minister to France in 1881 where he favored commissioning Bartholdi to make the Statue of Liberty. For this labor, he earned the honor of driving the first rivet into Lady Liberty's toe. He became governor of New York in 1895.

Morton's five daughters grew up on the family estate, Ellerslie, in yet another home built by society's architect Richard Morris Hunt. The house was near the Hyde Park residence of James and Sara Roosevelt. The Roosevelts and Mortons were close, not only as neighbors. They took trips to the Adirondacks and traveled to Europe together. Edith counted herself as one of FDR's oldest friends. After her marriage, Franklin often stopped at Corcoran House, her home in Washington, on his way to the Navy Department. Edith opened her doors to him and Lucy so they could meet away from prying eyes, and during World War II he relaxed in her home.

Edith was one of Consuelo Vanderbilt's bridesmaids. Alma Vanderbilt so controlled her daughter's wedding that she chose her daughter's eight bridesmaids Consuelo recalled, "from among her friends for her own reasons. . . ."

Edith's sister Helen also acquired a duke and heartache. She married the Duc de Valencan whom she met while her father was minister to France, but he was more interested in her six million dollar dowry. He deserted her shortly after the wedding, and the marriage was annulled. Afterwards she styled herself simply as Mrs. Helen Morton.

Edith also found her husband William Corcoran Eustis, known as "Willie," during her father's sojourn in France. She married the wealthy, sporting gentleman in 1901 and lived in Washington and Virginia horse country occupying the historic country house known as Oatlands, built in 1810.

Sister Alice, the youngest of the Morton sisters and known as the tallest and the fairest of the girls, also chose a wealthy sportsman for a husband in Winthrop Rutherfurd. Losing Consuelo had affected him. He did not marry Alice until he was forty years old in 1902, seven years after Consuelo became the Duchess of Marlborough.

Their fifteen years together were happy. Winthrop and Alice spent their time at the family estate Tranquility in Allamuchy, New Jersey, staying in New York City or Washington, D.C., and wintering in Aiken, South Carolina. They had six children, five sons: Lewis, Winthrop, Jr., John, Hugo, Guy, and one daughter, Alice. The family filled their days with the societal activities of the landed gentry—horses, dogs, parties, and travel. Their life together seemed marred only by an incident in 1907 when kidnappers threatened to abduct two of their sons from their Allamuchy home. When they added extra security at the estate, the Rutherfurds received no further threats.

Alice's death left the fifty-five-year-old Rutherfurd with six children, none of them out of their teens. Helen, who had married the French duke, built a Carmelite monastery in Brooklyn to immortalize her sister. Alice had converted to Catholicism before her death as had Rutherfurd. They raised their children in the Catholic faith. Winthrop had built his wife a small stone chapel at Allamuchy where a priest said mass on Sundays.

Both Helen and Edith Eustis were concerned for the future of their sister's brood. While they would never lack nurses, nannies, or tutors, they needed a mother. As a friend to both Lucy and Franklin and sister-in-law to Winthrop, did Edith play matchmaker? Franklin, of course, had known Alice, and would have felt genuine sorrow at her passing. He would always care for Lucy. After they parted, would he have spoken with his old friend Edith about Lucy needing a position in the world?

What is known is that Lucy and Winty were acquainted. They moved in the same circles, they knew the same people, and both needed what the other could offer.

* * *

Lucy could not take refuge in North Carolina forever. By 1919 she was living again with her mother in the Toronto Apartments in Washington and paying the thirty-five dollars a month rent. Her sister Violetta, the army nurse, was still abroad in France.

Huybertie "Bertie" Hamlin, inside observer of Washington society, wrote Jonathan Daniels,* author of *Washington Quadrille*, "Did not Miss M. go for a time to 'Tranquility' to try to smooth out the household and affairs of Alice Morton Rutherfurd? She had one girl and four boys all in a heap—one boy died later at Edith Eustis's house of pneumonia." From that came the idea often quoted by biographers and historians that Lucy went to Tranquility as governess to the Rutherfurd children.

Rutherfurd was a middle-aged widower with six children. He wanted and needed to be married. Lucy was younger, beautiful, elegant in his drawing room. She was also steadfast, for she stayed by Winthrop's side when his eldest son, Lewis, suffered a long illness during 1919. Having survived a hopeless love affair, Lucy wanted and needed some stability and security, and here was a large ready-made family. She didn't mind a large family,

*Daniels was the son of Josephus Daniels, the secretary of the navy and FDR's boss when he was assistant secretary of the navy. Jonathan Daniels became FDR's press secretary in 1945.

for Lucy had worked in the Roosevelt household of five children. Rutherfurd, although twice Lucy's age and a year older than her mother, was still a handsome and vital man. He was also a Catholic.* He also had a considerable fortune, although Lucy's cousin Mrs. Cotten always insisted, "She married Mr. Rutherfurd, *not* for money but because she felt he needed her."

How would Franklin feel about her intended nuptials? She wanted him to know of her plans, but she felt she could not contact him directly. She didn't want him to read it in the newspapers or hear it from others. Lucy phoned a mutual friend, Mrs. Frank Polk and asked her to "please tell Franklin" of her marriage plans. Polk had been undersecretary of state when Roosevelt was assistant secretary of the Navy. The Polks and Roosevelts socialized often. Over tea at the Roosevelts, Mrs. Polk tried without success to get Franklin aside to tell him of Lucy's news. In exasperation as she and her husband were leaving, she loudly told Eleanor of Lucy's engagement so that Franklin could not help but overhear it. He "started like a horse in fear of a hornet," but made no comment.

Lucy married Rutherfurd on Friday, February 13, 1920. His eldest son, Lewis, had died of pneumonia a few days prior to the wedding. The *Washington Post* reported:

> Mrs. Carroll Mercer announces the marriage of her daughter, Lucy Page, to Mr. Winthrop Rutherfurd of New York. The ceremony took place yesterday morning at the home of Dr. and Mrs. William B. Marbury, the latter a sister of the bride. On account of deep mourning, only immediate families were present.

Lucy's sister, Violetta, had married Dr. Marbury in 1919 on their return from France where she had served with him during the war. Like the Carrolls, Marbury came from an old, well-known Maryland family.

---

*According to Joseph Alsop author of *Centenary Remembrance*, Lucy's confessor urged her to marry Rutherfurd.

Newspapers did not print details of the wedding, not even the guest list, which was standard practice for a society wedding at that time. The *New York Times* did note, "Mr. and Mrs. Rutherfurd will leave immediately for the former's home at Allamuchy, N.J."

Minnie must have been relieved that both daughters were well married. Yet, two weeks following Lucy's marriage to a wealthy man, Minnie filed to increase her late husband's pension on which she depended for her living. Her attorney swore that she was "without resources of what kind soever." She had appealed to Senator George E. Chamberlain in January to help her with her claim "after filling out twenty-five or thirty papers."

The remaining Rutherfurd children would also have been present at their father's wedding ceremony. The *Journal of Society* did report that the Mortons were not happy that Rutherfurd "failed to tell his first wife's family of his intended marriage, and he hastened to have the knot tied a very short time after the death of a son." Despite this negative comment, certainly Edith Eustis favored the marriage as a friend to all involved. Elizabeth Henderson Cotten attended the ceremony with her impressionable eleven-year-old son whose main recollections were of his beautiful cousin Lucy marrying an "old and ugly" man and of the delicious wedding cake.

In a long letter dated February 14, 1920, Eleanor regaled her mother-in-law with casual chitchat about the children and politics. She ended her letter with a postscript, "Did you know Lucy Mercer married Mr. Wintie Rutherfurd two days ago?" Franklin may have been shocked, but Eleanor breathed a sigh of relief. Lucy seemed to be out of their lives.

* * *

After Lucy and he parted, Roosevelt made a concerted effort to be a devoted husband and family man. He came home earlier and spent more time with the children now between the ages three and thirteen. He changed his Sunday golf game to the afternoon to attend church "which I know is a great sacrifice to please me," Eleanor wrote Sara. As a second honeymoon, the two of them went to Europe in 1919 as Franklin managed the distribution of American military stores after the war. Eleanor toured French hospitals and battlefields. They saw old friends in England. She attended parties with her husband and left with him. Eleanor would never fully forgive him, but the couple did come to a truce, a working partnership to last the rest of the days of their marriage.

Lucy's departure caused Eleanor to contemplate her place in the world. Her maternal Grandmother Hall died in 1919, and now she questioned her grandmother's choices. "I wonder now whether, if her life had been less centered in her family group, that family group might not have been a great deal better off. If she had some kind of life of her own, what would have been the result?" Eleanor, who wanted a "life of her own," started repeating several sayings she would give as advice to others throughout her years, "The life you live is your own," and "Life is meant to be lived." No longer would she stand in the shadow of her mother-in-law, her husband, or anyone.

With the end of World War I, his love affair, and his marriage as he had known it, Roosevelt was a man ready for a career change. Woodrow Wilson's presidency was up in 1920, and Franklin had several choices. He wanted to be governor. "Once you're elected Governor of New York, if you do well enough in that job, you have a good show to be President. . . ." but the popular Al Smith was ensconced in that spot. He could run for senator from New York, but a better prize was the vice presidential nomination. At the Democratic convention in San Francisco, the Democratic Party was deeply divided on all major issues. It took forty-four ballots to nominate Governor

James M. Cox of Ohio as their candidate for president with Franklin D. Roosevelt as his running mate. Republicans were confident of winning the election in the aftermath of the demobilization and disillusionment that followed the war. Americans were tired of shortages and high prices. They'd had enough of internationalism and weren't interested in Woodrow Wilson's League of Nations, a precursor to the United Nations. The Republican Party nominated Senator Warren G. Harding of Ohio with Calvin Coolidge as vice president. Harding promoted "normalcy" and that is what the American people wanted in 1920.

For the first time women, including Lucy Rutherfurd and Eleanor Roosevelt, could vote nationally in an election, and the Republicans sought women voters. Harding followed the platform of the League of Women Voters and adopted such stands as equal pay for equal work and the appointment of more women to public office. The Democrats pushed the League of Nations. FDR, who would be a staunch supporter of the United Nations toward the end of his life, agreed with Wilson and Cox to put it at the center of his campaign.

Roosevelt didn't expect to win the election. What he did win was the experience of campaigning around the country, giving speeches, networking with other politicians, gaining national attention, and a taste for more. When the votes were counted, the Republicans not only won the White House but also big majorities in Congress. Even Al Smith lost his seat as governor of New York to the Republican conservative Nathan L. Miller who did not favor women's suffrage.

Franklin Roosevelt entered private life first as an attorney, but bored by "estates, wills, etc.," he then became a different type of vice president, that of Fidelity and Deposit, a surety bonding firm. He dabbled in merchandizing such as putting advertising in taxicabs, and he waited to run for the United States Senate in 1922.

In 1921 he was tested physically as he had been emotionally in 1918. At Campobello that summer, he felt tired and ached all over. His left leg "lagged" when he tried to get out of bed. "I tried to persuade myself that the trouble with my leg was muscular, that it would disappear as I used it. But presently it refused to work, and then the other."

When his temperature reached 102 degrees, a local doctor diagnosed a cold. A vacationing specialist Dr. Keen thought it to be a blood clot and prescribed leg massages when even touching the sheets covering his legs sent Roosevelt into agony. Soon Roosevelt's legs were not only numb, he couldn't stand. "By the end of the third day practically all muscles from the chest down were involved," stated Roosevelt. The Boston specialist Dr. Robert W. Lovett declared Roosevelt to be a victim of poliomyelitis, infantile paralysis. A man of nearly forty had succumbed to what many considered a child's disease.* While mainly children were struck by the polio virus, it also could infect adults. A healthy person not under stress had the best chance of resisting, but in Eleanor's words her husband had, "had no real rest since the war," nor was he free from stress. The loss of Lucy was difficult enough, but after the war and prior to his run for the vice presidency, policies at the Department of the Navy came under fire from the Senate Naval Committee. Roosevelt and Daniels were accused first of making the naval prison at Portsmouth more pleasant than life at sea and then of using entrapment to clean up the Newport, Rhode Island, naval base of homosexuals. Roosevelt denied the charges, asked for a Congressional investigation, and diverted the potential damage to his political career.

*FDR and Eleanor feared their children would contact the disease. They allowed the children only to come to the door of the sickroom once a day during the first weeks of his illness.

What started as a routine summer vacation had become what Eleanor later called "a trial by fire." She placed a cot in her husband's bedroom and nursed him around the clock for three weeks. FDR, paralyzed from the waist down, was totally dependent on his wife. She bathed and fed him, shaved him, and brushed his teeth. She also administered enemas and placed a catheter through his penis to his bladder. She had to turn the dead weight of his body to keep him from getting bedsores. Roosevelt's political advisor, Louis Howe moved in and was her only relief caretaker.*

The vigorous massages prescribed by Dr. Keen exhausted her and sadly worsened the paralysis. Dr. Lovett stopped this practice that left FDR in torturous pain and Eleanor in deep guilt. For Keen's worthless advice he charged six hundred dollars. FDR later admitted that those early days of his illness left him "in utter despair . . . fearing that God had abandoned him."

Roosevelt's mother did not know of the seriousness of her son's illness until she returned from Europe in September. As she stated to her brother:

> His legs (that I have always been proud of) have to be moved often as they ache when long in one position. He and Eleanor decided at once to be cheerful and the atmosphere of the house is all happiness, so I have fallen in and follow their glorious example.

Wife, mother, children all followed the "glorious example." James remembered, ". . . Father was unbelievably concerned about how we would take it. He grinned at us, and he did his best to call out, or gasp out, some cheery response to our tremulous, just-this-side-of-tears greeting." The glorious example of smiling through all adversity took its toll. Eleanor realized her mother-in-law, "out of sight . . . wept many hours but with all of us she was very cheerful."

---

*Louis Howe never left the Roosevelt household, including the White House, until his death in 1936.

Eleanor, herself, broke down in April 1922, while she was reading to five-year-old Johnnie and seven-year-old Franklin, Jr. She "sobbed and sobbed" for hours and no one could comfort her until "Eventually I pulled myself together. . . ." She would later recall this as "the one and only time" in her life when she lost control and went to pieces. She would eventually see Franklin's illness as a "blessing in disguise" for it built his character, that it changed him from a slightly self-absorbed man into a serious person who could truly care about the adversity of others. Their son James disagreed, "I believe that he was at heart a humanitarian who did not have to be crippled to care about others. In short, I do not think . . . that the ordeal of being crippled built father's character. I believe he had the basic strength of character to overcome his handicap."

Sara wanted her son to retire to Springwood at Hyde Park, to live the life of a country squire as his father had. Eleanor and Louis Howe knew he would not so easily give up politics. It seemed impossible for voters to elect a disabled man in a wheelchair to any office. It is difficult to imagine today how society viewed the handicapped in the 1920s. If paralytic patients survived the beginning phases of their disease, for most died of infections, medicine could do little for them. Options for therapy or drugs were few. Often families hid the handicapped at home or warehoused them in the few rehabilitative hospitals in the United States. People feared or ridiculed them believing that a physical defect indicated moral or intellectual defects. "Mainstreaming" was an unknown concept.

No one outside of the family was to know what struck Roosevelt. "Mother told us not to talk about polio, as so many people were scared of it," Anna recalled. Howe released the first story on Roosevelt's illness in late August of 1921. It simply stated that the former vice-presidential candidate was recuperating from a serious illness and a full recovery was expected.

During the winter of 1921, Roosevelt regained the control of his body functions, and the muscular strength of his arms returned.

He believed that one day he would walk again. "I'm not going to be conquered by a childish disease," he declared. The next seven years, from 1921 until 1928, Roosevelt worked on his recuperation and rehabilitation. His mother did have him at Hyde Park several months each year, but he sought water treatments at Cape Cod, Massachusetts, in Florida, and at Warm Springs, Georgia. With intense, daily physical therapy, he strengthened his arms and back, so he could swing in and out of a wheelchair. He was confident he would soon be on crutches and "walking without any limp." By February 1922 he was on crutches with the aid of braces. He could stand. He moved by swinging his hips. He worked on building the muscles in his legs, but he would never walk on his own again not even with a limp.

While FDR worked on rehabilitating his body, Eleanor and Louis Howe worked on rehabilitating his political career. Following Howe's advice, she became involved in the Democratic Party to keep the party interested in her husband. She worked in both Dutchess County and New York state politics. The two persuaded Al Smith to provide FDR with a political coming out in 1924. He would give the nominating speech putting Al Smith's name forward as the party's candidate for president.*

With his sixteen-year-old son James behind him, FDR in locked steel braces weighing fourteen pounds and on crutches had to make the Sisyphean fifteen feet to the podium by himself to give his speech. "I never in my life was as proud of father as I was at that moment" James wrote. Placing a crutch forward, shifting his weight toward the crutch, then moving the other crutch, shifting again, he began his "walk" down the campaign trail that would lead him to the White House.

---

*The Democrats nominated a compromise candidate, John W. Davis, who was defeated by Calvin Coolidge. Smith did win reelection as governor of New York against Republican Theodore Roosevelt, Jr.

CHAPTER 8

"I hear that you are a grandfather"

Life changed irrevocably for Lucy Rutherfurd in the years known as the Roaring Twenties just as it had for Franklin and Eleanor Roosevelt. Women may have shortened their skirts, bobbed their long hair, danced the Charleston, and called themselves flappers, but being a wife to Winty and a mother to his five children filled Lucy's days. The Jazz Age may have been frenzied, but it was legally dry because of Prohibition. Harry Houdini entertained crowds with his seemingly impossible magical escapes. Henry Ford's mass production put affordable Model Ts on the American road. Charlie Chaplin was on the screen and Amelia Earhardt in the air. Through it all Lucy was at home in Tranquility.

Tranquility at Allamuchy was a fitting name for the farm to which Lucy and Winthrop retreated as newlyweds. Ironically, Eleanor Roosevelt was fond of quoting, "Back of tranquility lies always conquered unhappiness" from the popular book, *The Countryman's Year.* Lucy had indeed conquered her unhappiness. She had a handsome, wealthy husband who adored her and five robust stepchildren. After being married over a year, she became pregnant. She gave birth in 1922 at the age of thirty-one to her only child, a daughter she named Barbara.

Allamuchy Township and the mountain in northwestern New Jersey were named after the chief of the Lenape Indians, Allamuchahokkingen meaning, "place within the hills." The Rutherfurd land had been in the family since the 1780s and had grown to over eight thousand acres and contained five farms.* The main house, in the style of an English manor house, had been built by Rutherfurd for his first wife. The thirty-five-room mansion was several miles from the older Rutherfurd house. It sat among a thousand acres of forests, a private lake, a rose garden, and its own golf course. Crops flourished on the fertile land, and the acreage produced hay for Winty's Holstein cattle. The Morris Canal shipped coal, iron, and lime east to manufacturers. Winty's kennels boasted champion smooth fox terriers. In an era when laborers made thirty to fifty cents an hour, he willingly paid $1500 for a dog to strengthen his kennel's bloodlines. Respected for his knowledge as a dog breeder, he served as a judge of fox and Irish terriers for both the American Kennel Club and the Westminster Kennel Club.

Despite that Rutherfurd often employed as many as five professional gardeners, Lucy insisted on having her own private plot for her garden. Here she could work planting and weeding among her roses and other flowers in her large gardener's hat to shield her face and her French kid gloves to protect her hands. Winty valued those parts of anatomy.

As with the first Mrs. Rutherfurd, Lucy was not only mistress of Tranquility but also of homes in New York and Washington,

*Today, land from the Rutherfurd-Stuyvesant estate makes up Allamuchy Mountain State Park. Environmentalists and preservationists would also like to preserve Tranquility Farm.

but it was in Aiken, South Carolina, where the Rutherfurds were at the forefront of society life, and it was there that Lucy came into her own.

Aiken, located 170 miles northwest of Charleston near the Georgia and South Carolina border, first came to prominence as a summer retreat from "the heat and malaria of unhealthier regions" of Charleston and low country plantations. The area's history, of course, preceded the founding of the city of Aiken. Hernando DeSoto was the first European in the area when he crossed the Savannah River looking for gold and silver. The Cofachiqui Indians unwisely welcomed him and his men into South Carolina. When he did not find the precious metals he wanted, he stole what goods the Cofachiqui had, including their Queen Cacique, and left. The English settled in the area in 1685. By the 1830s the area needed better transportation to export its cotton and tobacco crops. William Aiken, a wealthy cotton merchant and president of the South Carolina and Railroad Company, hired Horatio Allen, who was later a consultant on building the Brooklyn Bridge, to build a railroad from Charleston to Hamburg, South Carolina. The railroad tracks followed the same trade routes of the Creek and Chickasaw Indians. The train, known as the "Best Friend," was the first locomotive made for regular rail service in the United States. On October 2, 1833, it arrived at Aiken, named for the railway president. By 1835 the town received its charter from the state.

General William Tecumseh Sherman's "march to the sea" was a scorched earth progress across Georgia to the Atlantic coast in an effort to cut the South in half and bring about an end to the Civil War or, as known in South Carolina, the War between the States. Sherman's army cut a sixty-mile swath of burned homes and crops and seized livestock to bring the South to its knees. On December 10, 1864, Sherman and his men reached Savannah. He declared it his "Christmas gift" for Lincoln.

After a month in Savannah, Sherman turned to South Carolina. He would deal harshly with the "cradle of secession." In his words, "When I go through South Carolina, it will be one of the most horrible things in the history of the world. The devil himself couldn't restrain my men in that state."

Despite his boasts, Sherman's army received a rare defeat from Confederate Major General Joseph Wheeler's cavalry at Aiken. Wheeler turned back Sherman's raiders headed by Brigadier General Hugh Kilpatrick on February 11, 1865. Sherman and his men then turned toward Columbia capturing it a week later and burning two-thirds of the city. The Battle of Aiken spared the town this fate, and the city annually celebrates the battle complete with a reenactment.

After the war, wealthy northerners discovered Aiken as a health resort with its climate and springs. By 1869, Aiken's inns and boarding houses were turning away twice as many visitors as they could accommodate. Many of these "northern sojourners" liked Aiken so much that they built lavish homes attracting artisans and workers from all over the country to decorate those homes. A town that had started as a summer resort for southerners, now became the "Winter Colony" for Knickerbocker society who declared it "smart." The natives of Aiken liked to say they, "Lived on Yankees in the winter, and blackberries in the summer."

The wealthy newcomers brought their love of equestrian sports with them. They played the first outdoor polo match in America in 1882 making Aiken the center of the polo world for a time. The mild winter climate lured Northern horse breeders to ship their horses from New York to Aiken for training. Generally, the social season followed the thoroughbred migration. The horses arrived in October and left in the spring to return north for the racing season. Hitchcock Woods, a preserve of two thousand acres donated by the prominent Hitchcock family and located in the center of Aiken, hosted horse shows, drag hunts where riders and hounds chased a scent and not a real fox, and riding trails. Where people ride, they also play golf. The Palmetto Golf Club, founded in 1882, added to the recreational facilities of Aiken and gave it yet another title, "Sports Center of the South."

Those who frequented Aiken over the years read like a roster from society's *Who's Who*. William K. and Alma Vanderbilt had a winter home in Aiken. Alice Roosevelt Longworth, the Astors, the Mellons, and even the Duke and Duchess of Windsor, visited Aiken in the winter. It was also for a time the home of the Hope Diamond.

Evalyn Walsh McLean who liked to say, "I cannot help it if I have a passion for jewels," owned the forty-five-and-a-half-carat infamous diamond. Evalyn's love of gems started early. When her wealthy father asked what it would take for her to change what he considered an outrageous teenage hairstyle, she replied, "Jewelry!"

Evalyn, whose father made his money mining gold, married Edward Beale McLean, whose father owned the *Cincinnati Enquirer* and the *Washington Post*. The couple entertained lavishly in Washington, and they were acquaintances of the Rutherfurds and the Roosevelts. In the winter, they went to Aiken as did so many of their social peers. Mrs. McLean once phoned her Aiken neighbor to go to her winter home, Dinsmore Cottage, and look in the gramophone horn. There her neighbor found the Hope diamond wrapped in newspaper just where Mrs. Walsh had left it. This was not the only place where Mrs. Walsh kept her magnificent diamond. At home in Washington, D.C., she displayed the steely blue gem, which had once adorned the neck of King Louis IV of France, on the collar of her Great Dane, Max.

The Rutherfurds, with their wealth and family credentials, fit perfectly into Aiken's social circles. Lucy and Winty, the Rutherfurd children, and the new baby, came to Aiken to escape the harsh winters of New York and New Jersey. Like so many before them, they turned to Mrs. Eulalie Chafee Salley to find them a home.

Mrs. Salley was a determined suffragette who organized Aiken's South Carolina Equal Suffrage League. Although married to an attorney who was the mayor of Aiken, she practiced what she preached and wanted her own income. She once said, "Limiting me to domestic responsibility was like hitching a race horse to a plow." She turned to real estate in 1916 and established Eulalie Salley and Company. She prided herself on her company's motto, "We do everything but brush your teeth."* It made her the realtor for the Winter Colony. When her clients bought houses from her, she wanted a completed home for the new owners when they put the key in the front door. She decorated the houses, readied the gardens, and even hired servants for her customers. Mrs. Salley's gardener Bamberg had recently married, and Mrs. Salley hired his wife, Emma, to cook for the Rutherfurds.

Mrs. Salley first found a large rental stucco house for Lucy, Winty, and family. The three-story home had seven bedrooms, five bathrooms, and four rooms for servants. The Rutherfurds were only in the residence a few months when it burned. They turned again to Mrs. Salley, and this time she found them a smaller dwelling on Hayne Avenue. Here they stayed while they built a house on Berrie Road across from the Palmetto Golf Club where Winty played golf and served as chairman of the greens committee.

Winty was particularly adamant about fireproofing his new home, Ridgeley Hall II. Not only had their first rented home in Aiken burned, but fire also destroyed a barn at Tranquility. Five fire companies from nearby towns could not save sixty-five tons of hay.

---

*Her company still proudly sells real estate in Aiken today.

Ironically, the first Ridgeley Hall built in 1901 burned in 1926. Gussie Gardner, an old friend of Franklin Roosevelt, had owned the house and land. Augustus P. Gardner of Boston was a congressional representative who supported the young Roosevelt's unpopular desire to build up the navy prior to America's entrance into World War I. Roosevelt's determination in the face of President Wilson's neutrality made him declare, "I admire the courage of Franklin Roosevelt." Gussie rushed into uniform in 1918 to see action in World War I, but he died of pneumonia before he could go overseas.

In yet another example of how small the world can be among the socially prominent, the Rutherfurds hired architect Julian Peabody to build their new house. Peabody was the son-in-law of Thomas and Louise Eustis Hitchcock. Louise Eustis was the sister of Willis Eustis whose Washington home had been open to FDR and Lucy by his wife Edith, sister of Alice, the first Mrs. Winthrop Rutherfurd.

Peabody had Ridgeley Hall rebuilt with Winty's fear of fire in mind.* Constructed with red brick, its structure consisted of steel reinforced concrete and topped with a slate roof. It was finished in 1929. The Georgian style mansion contained fourteen bedrooms and fourteen bathrooms.

Aiken considered the Rutherfurds a "stunning couple." They would never suffer "the Aiken frost" reserved for outsiders without the proper social connections. Palmetto Golf Club had even prevented President-elect William Howard Taft from playing a round of golf because, "We don't really know Mr. Taft."

Aiken saw Winty as "delightful" but "austere" and jealous of any attention his wife might show anyone else including his own

*Sadly, the Rutherfurds seemed cursed to suffer fires. The last remaining building of Tranquility in New Jersey burned in 1984. It had been part of Garden State Academy, a Christian high school.

children. Mrs. Salley remembered, "He was desperately in love with her. He kissed her every time he saw her." To Lucy's neighbors and friends she was a refined woman "who looked even more beautiful as you got closer to her" and "perfectly devoted in every way to her husband." While the Rutherfurd children participated in all the sports Aiken had to offer, Lucy and Winty preferred a quieter life, seldom entertaining and only going out occasionally in the evening.

While Lucy seemed settled in Aiken, her spirit still haunted Franklin and Eleanor Roosevelt. In 1923, five years after Lucy had left their lives, their daughter Anna learned of the romance. At the age of sixty Anna wrote:

> When I was 17, in 1923, an elderly, gossipy cousin of my mother told me Father had had a romance with "another woman" during World War I in Washington; that many people had talked about it at the time and that it was all very hard on my mother; but that there had never been any question of a divorce and the "talk" had quickly died down.

Anna's reaction to the news was sympathy for her mother and recognition of the previous two years of hardship caused by her father's illness and her mother's fight to hold the family together. Those years, "had deepened my respect and understanding of both my parents." Six months later Eleanor told Anna everything: her ill father's return from Europe, Lucy's discovered letters, Eleanor's offer of a divorce, and when the family stayed intact, her insistence that her husband sever the relationship forever.*

Despite the promise from Franklin to have no other contact with Lucy, a cheery letter dated April 16, 1927, survives from her. It shows no trace that this is their first contact in nearly ten years. Written on stationery embossed "Aiken, South Carolina," it begins, "Dear Franklin, I hear that you are a grandfather—although

*Anna's brothers did not learn of their father's romance until after his death.

I do not know exactly just what one's feelings are on that question. Still I am sure, in your case, it's a subject of congratulation for all concerned." The lighthearted, friendly tone of the letter acknowledging the birth of daughter Anna's first child born in March, suggests that communication between the two had not ceased.*

Lucy goes on to mention, "I was interested to hear a little about you and your projects from Livy Davis who was here." Livingston Davis had attended Harvard with FDR and had worked as Roosevelt's assistant in the Navy Department, so he was a friend of Lucy's as well. He had often joined Lucy, FDR, and others on their excursions when Eleanor and the children were at Campobello. He, like Nigel Law, had served as Lucy's escort. Eleanor had never liked Livy or his drinking or womanizing. She called him "lazy, selfish."

Lucy's letter relays that she'd had a "miserable winter, but am much better." She further informs FDR that the family is going abroad in the summer and the children are very excited about the trip. She further hopes that the children "will get it out of their systems for several years to come."

From the *S.S. Belgenland* on July 2, 1927, she writes again, "You see we are off on our first extended family jaunt. . . . The children have all enjoyed it every second and it is a great pleasure for me to find them all entertained without having to lift a finger. . . ."

A more intriguing part of the letter concerns her news to Franklin that her friends the Kittredges have sold "their place" which left "still unsold the tract the Boy Scouts were considering."

---

*Anna had married stockbroker Curtis Dall in 1926. They named their first child Anna Eleanor, nicknamed "Sistie." They also had a son named Curtis or "Buzzie." Both were the darlings of Washington press during their grandfather's first term as president, 1932–1936.

She adds that she has heard "you had found a better place somewhere else, and though I am sorry to hear it. Still it may be best in the end. . . ." As this was the same time that Roosevelt was buying land around Warm Springs, Georgia, it sounds as if he had considered buying something in Aiken closer to her. She encourages Franklin and Eleanor to travel abroad and relates how the invalid sister of Bessie Kittredge was able to travel overseas in a specially made chair "that would fit easily in French trains." She thinks the chair collapsible and is willing to find out more about it if her old friend would be interested.

Although FDR had spent seven years trying to recover the use of his legs, he was still wearing braces, "walking" with a cane in one hand, and gripping the arm of his son or someone else so he would not appear crippled in public. Throughout his political career, he and his political advisor Louis Howe admonished the press not to photograph him sitting in a wheelchair or locking his braces in place when he alighted from an automobile. "No movies of me getting out of the machine, boys," he would tell the newsreel cameramen. So successful was he in this illusion that of the over 35,000 photos of him in the Franklin Delano Roosevelt Presidential Library only two exist with him in a wheelchair. Most Americans did not know he was paraplegic until after his death.

Lucy ends her letter with the offer to do any errands on the continent or in England he might need and with the hope that she doesn't come home "to find you President or Sec'y [*sic*] of State nor yet a physical wreck from too much work for Al Smith or any other potentate!!"

Lucy would come home to find Smith chosen by the Democrats as their presidential candidate only to be defeated by Herbert Hoover in the 1928 elections, and Roosevelt running for governor of New York. Roosevelt, of course, won; he was the potentate.

CHAPTER 9

"Mr. President"

When the Rutherfurds were at home in Allamuchy, Mr. Danks, the farm manager of Tranquility, stood once a week at the desk of Winthrop Rutherfurd. His employer always asked the same question, "How is the farm?" In 1929 the answers were not good; prices were falling.

The conclusion of World War I planted the seeds of the Great Depression. In the Treaty of Versailles that ended the hostilities, the Allies punished Germany for starting the war. In addition to taking Germany's colonies and reducing its military power, the victors wanted Germany to pay the monetary cost of the war. Germany borrowed money from the United States to pay reparations to Britain and France who, in turn, paid that money to the United States as part of their war debt. A war-ravaged Europe did not have the resources to buy from the United States, so they borrowed more.

Countries lived on speculation and so did their citizens. In the United States, as the stock market rose, everyone wanted to invest. Those without the money bought stocks on margin by only putting up a portion of the cost of an already overpriced stock. Money went into speculation but not production or purchasing. When the crash came on Black Thursday, October 24, those who'd invested but didn't have the money were now left with stocks worth nothing. No money, no buying power, no employment—the vicious cycle of the Great Depression had begun. Before it was over about one fourth of the American workforce, eleven million people, were unemployed and many banks and businesses failed.

Rutherfurd had the money to weather the storm even if the value of livestock and crops on his farms fell. He could pay his everyday bills, but most farmers couldn't, and they had outstanding bank loans. The good times of the 1920s had bypassed the poor, many of whom were tenant farmers and sharecroppers. In 1930, Congress passed the Hawley-Smoot bill, which mandated a high tariff on imported goods. Everyone, including farmers, now paid higher prices for items manufactured abroad. Worse, foreign countries retaliated with their own tariffs. Overseas markets for U.S. goods and crops dried up. Weather conditions worsened the situation as drought in the Midwest lead to the dust bowl and plagues of grasshoppers devoured all in their path from fence posts to the washing on the clothesline. When banks foreclosed on farms, many like the Joads of John Steinbeck's *The Grapes of Wrath* declared, "A man got to do what he got to do," and left for California.

Americans elected Herbert Hoover in a time of optimism. Now he faced one of the most pessimistic eras of United States history. He favored little intervention from the federal government to help the American economy. His critics chastised him for not being able to alleviate problems far beyond his influence, and they unfairly blamed him for a crisis no one could have averted. In the ultimate insult, those who'd lost their jobs and homes, stood in breadlines, and ate at soup kitchens now lived in shanties in makeshift towns they called "Hoovervilles."

Hoover's administration did try some relief efforts. It set up the Emergency Committee for Employment, passed the Home Loan Bank Act to loan money so people could keep their homes, and put in place the Reconstruction Finance Corporation to lend money to banks, railroads, and businesses.

Franklin Roosevelt as governor of New York became prominent nationally for his efforts to help the small farmer. During the four years that he served two, two-year terms, FDR was a progressive governor. He initiated tax relief for farmers, and in an era when not everyone had electricity, he advocated cheaper electric power for all. He wanted unemployment insurance to help those out of work until they found jobs. He established the Temporary Emergency Relief Administration for financially suffering New York workers and their families. In many of these programs were the ideas that would come to fruition during his presidency.

By 1932 the man who had promised, "Two chickens in every pot and a car in every garage" was doomed to be a one-term president. Hoover's caution had not impressed Americans, and it had not helped the country's economic difficulties. On the contrary, Roosevelt's jaunty smile and positive demeanor inspired confidence for many voters. In his acceptance speech as the Democratic Party's presidential candidate, he pledged himself to "a new deal for the American people." His New Deal would include regulating stock sales, starting public works, reforesting projects, controlling crop productions, lowering the tariff, refinancing farm and home mortgages.

To counter any questions about his health, Roosevelt conducted a "whistle-stop" campaign. In each town, Roosevelt with the help of his eldest son, James, would step out onto the last car of the train. Smiling he would say, "I am just out here to look, learn and listen." He would introduce other members of his family, James's wife, Betsey, and his daughter Anna. Then he would joke, "And this is my little boy James. I have more hair than he has." The laughing crowd saw a vibrant, self-assured man. After a few more words and campaign pledges, the train left the station for the next stop.

When the polls closed and the votes counted, Roosevelt carried forty-two states and 472 electoral votes to Hoover's six states and fifty-nine electoral votes. The country had to wait four months for Roosevelt to make good on his promises. The passage of the Twentieth Amendment to the Constitution changed the inauguration of the president from March 4 to January 20. In his second term, Roosevelt became the first president inaugurated on January 20, 1937.

On the eve of his inauguration, it looked as if worried depositors might make a run on banks and withdraw all their money. Still governor, Roosevelt declared a two-day holiday closing all New York banks. Governors of eighteen other states followed his example, and the nation averted a banking crisis. The Banking Relief Act of March 9 approved the bank holidays, which gave governmental agencies time to inspect banks, reopen the sound ones, and reestablish confidence in the country's banking system.* Roosevelt explained his actions and reassured the American public with his first radio "fireside chat" on March 12. The journalist Walter Lippman wrote, "In one week, the nation, which had lost confidence in everything and everybody, has regained confidence in the government and in itself."

March 4, 1933, dawned a gray, chilly day to match the apprehensive mood of the nation. At noon Franklin Roosevelt's family, his wife, mother, and children, watched as FDR took the oath of office as administered by Chief Justice Charles Evan Hughes. As he swore to "preserve, protect, and defend the Constitution of the

*It is difficult for modern readers to imagine banks failing, but the Federal Deposit Insurance Corporation, the FDIC, which insures bank deposits, did not come into being until 1933.

United States," he held his right hand on the three-hundred-year-old Dutch Bible of his ancestor Claes Martenswzen Van Rosenvelt. In attendance at this inauguration as she would be at all four of his inaugurations, unknown to Eleanor, was Lucy.* It had all been arranged through the help of yet another woman charmed by Franklin Roosevelt, Marguerite "Missy" LeHand.

She earned the nickname "Missy" because young Franklin, Jr. and John Roosevelt found it difficult to say "Miss LeHand." Missy became FDR's personal secretary at the insistence of Eleanor in 1921 after working first at the Democratic political headquarters when FDR was running for the vice presidency. Born in 1899, she was only twenty-one when she entered Franklin Roosevelt's life. Like so many women, he captivated her. She would remain his devoted secretary, confidant, hostess, and surrogate wife all of her life. White House aide Raymond Moley described her "as close to being a wife as he ever had—or could have."

Missy was pretty, witty, highly efficient, and utterly devoted to her employer, but Eleanor did not seem to mind the secretary's close proximity, personally and mentally, to her husband. "Though she did not come to live with us until we went to Albany [1928], she often stayed with us in Warm Springs and in Hyde Park, and was devoted to my husband and his work," Eleanor said of her. In reality, it was always Missy with FDR at Warm Springs or on the houseboat, the *Larocco*, or at Hyde Park when Eleanor was away. Missy's devotion to FDR freed Eleanor to act as his "legs" to travel and report what she found in order to advise him. She preferred an independent life to sitting by his

*In *Washington Quadrille*, Jonathan Daniels cited a source who stated that Lucy also attended Roosevelt's nomination for a third term as president at the Democratic Convention at Madison Square Garden in New York City in October 1940 (p. 282).

side. It was up to Missy to take on the daily chores of a wife: paying the bills, planning the menus, overseeing the children, ordering the house cleaned. Like Louis Howe, Missy would live with the Roosevelts at the governor's mansion and at the White House until felled by her debilitating stroke. From the beginning, Missy stood by her boss even when he physically couldn't stand. During the early days of his bout with polio, she took dictation several hours a day as he responded to personal and political mail. When he went in search of a cure for his paralysis, Missy was often with him whether on a houseboat or later at Warm Springs. Eleanor always considered Warm Springs to be Missy's domain. When Eleanor visited Warm Springs, which was seldom as she disliked its informality, she was the guest, for it was Missy who acted as hostess organizing the guests, activities, and menus, and presiding at the dinner table.

In February 1924, FDR cruised around Florida in a houseboat he bought with his Harvard friend John Lawrence, the *Larooco*, the name taken from Lawrence, Roosevelt & Company. Despite that the seventy-one-foot boat needed painting and it leaked, FDR enjoyed the fishing and swimming which he thought strengthened his legs. He relished the casual company of his invited friends. "All wander around in pajamas, nighties and bathing suits!" he wrote his mother. Eleanor disliked the climate, the company, the seasickness, the insects. For her the ocean "seemed eerie and menacing to me." As with Warm Springs, the relaxed lifestyle, which included alcohol, was not for her. Despite the country was under Prohibition until the Twenty-First Amendment repealed it in February 1933, Roosevelt served alcohol for he liked his cocktail time, which he called "the children's hour." He continued this practice through his White House days. At the Little White House in Warm Springs, Missy did the serving; at the White House in Washington, Roosevelt enjoyed mixing the drinks. Old fashioneds were a favorite, and he was known to make "wicked" martinis.

In a measure of FDR's trust of Missy, it was only to her on board the boat did he reveal his despair over his condition. "There were days on the *Larooco* when it was noon before he could pull himself out of depression and greet his guests wearing his lighthearted façade," she told Frances Perkins, Roosevelt's secretary of labor.* Only she called him "F.D." She happily worked with him on his stamp collection, something Eleanor never did. They shared jokes that no one else could understand, and she doted unashamedly. "She watches her man so closely that she can see the slightest changes in his emotional attitude before they have become apparent to anyone else," noted a journalist.

During Roosevelt's search for relief from his paralysis from 1925–1928, he spent nearly half of his time away from home. Missy spent most of that time with him despite her weak heart. Eleanor knew that Missy "had had rheumatic fever as a child. While she could ride and drive and swim, the more strenuous forms of exercise were forbidden." Eleanor worried that overwork would make Missy ill, which eventually happened.

Missy's closeness to her son did not escape Sara Roosevelt, and she disliked Missy's constant presence just as she resented Louis Howe. When Franklin stayed at Springwood, Missy stayed off the property. Eleanor often kept from her mother-in-law how often Missy was around. When Missy returned from her father's funeral on February 24, 1924, Eleanor didn't rush to tell her mother-in-law that Missy was back on the *Larooco*. She wrote her husband, "I think she has more peace of mind when she doesn't know things!" The children were often equally putout by Missy's constant attendance on their father. She irritated Franklin, Jr. by always agreeing with his father. He reduced her to tears by saying, "Don't you ever get mad and flare up? Do you always

*Perkins was the first woman named to a Cabinet position.

smile?" Elliott went so far as to write in his book that he thought his father and Missy were lovers because he had seen her dressed in her bathrobe on his father's lap on board the *Larooco*, and because she had quarters close to his in the governor's mansion and at the White House. Anna called her "the office wife, quote, unquote." Anna, James, and Franklin, Jr. felt nothing was going on beyond Missy's utter devotion and their father's need of her constant attention.

Missy had boyfriends. Earl Miller, Eleanor Roosevelt's bodyguard, dated Missy for two years, but he also saw other women on the White House staff and claimed that he only dated Missy because of her closeness to Franklin. Eleanor's friends thought that she was as besotted of Miller as FDR was of Missy. Even son James thought, "I believe there may have been one real romance in mother's life outside of marriage. Mother may have had an affair with Earl Miller. . . ."

Miller later admitted that his involvement with Missy was for Eleanor's sake. "When I heard that story of Lucy Mercer my heart went out to her—that he should have hurt her so." He said, "I played up to Missy—carried on an affair with her for two years." "My main purpose in playing up to Missy was because I knew the lady [his nickname for Eleanor] was being hurt." He married twice, in 1932 and 1941, to divert rumors about him and Eleanor, for as her bodyguard he was always with her. How involved these two were may never be known. Their relationship is even more allusive than that of FDR and Lucy. All that remains of the friendship of Eleanor and Miller are some photographs, home movies, and hints of a huge correspondence no one has found, if it still exists.

Lillian Rogers Parks, a White House maid, chronicled the perplexing associations of the occupants of the White House, "Missy was going to try to have a life of her own away from FDR. For a time she dated Earl Miller, who we heard was romantically involved with Eleanor. . . ." She goes on, "Missy also dated the wealthy William Bullitt, whom FDR made the first Ambassador to Russia and later appointed Ambassador to France." The staff speculated, ". . . if FDR engineered these romances so Missy would see how much better off she was with him." Her final comment echoes the sentiments of legions of biographers and historians, "It gave us a lot to think about."

Miller, like his "Lady," believed in helping the "underdog." In a move of great irony, Roosevelt asked him to accompany Lucy on an inspection of prisons in Georgia and Florida. As a society matron of Aiken, Lucy had both the time and money for philanthropic projects. Eleanor probably did not hear of this mission from FDR or Miller. Neither would have wanted to remind her of Lucy Mercer. During his journeys with Lucy, Miller remained loyal to Eleanor remarking that he thought Lucy "copied" Eleanor sounding "like her former boss" and having the same ideas and questions, for she was "quite the 'all-out' worker & giver of her time & money to many underprivileged." Together they worked to abolish sweatboxes in Florida and Georgia, used to punish prisoners, "after that boy died . . . for not saying *'sir'* to his White Trash Guard." Lucy wrote Miller saying that "she was proud that she was part of it." Miller saw Lucy as a pale imitation of Eleanor, "A person could just *not* be associated with the Lady without much of her 'do-good' rubbed off on you."

Miller may have been dating Missy for the sake of his boss, but William Bullitt wanted to marry her. According to James Roosevelt, "Father encouraged it, feeling, I think she had devoted a lot of her life to him and was entitled to a life of her own." When Bullitt also saw other women, Missy ended it only to remark years later to a friend that she did not regret marrying because, "How could anyone ever come up to FDR?"

Did Eleanor feel apprehensive about Missy? She knew no one could take the place of Lucy in Franklin's heart. Their marriage had weathered that storm and survived. James Roosevelt surmised about his father, "After his forced break with Lucy in 1918, and after he became crippled in 1921, she filled a need and made him feel a man again, which mother did not do." James described Missy in words similar to those who knew Lucy, "She had a sweet temper and nothing seemed to ruffle her. Missy pampered and flattered father. In fact, mother occasionally complained how Missy did whatever father wanted without questions. If Missy considered father infallible, mother did not."

Missy was not as dangerous to Eleanor as Lucy. Missy came from a different social class. Unlike Lucy, Missy's family was not only poor, but she had "no background at all" according to Margaret "Daisy" Suckley, yet another woman who shared a mysterious intimacy with FDR. Yet Missy's friends remembered, "She stood out for having a better appearance and being smarter than most." Like Lucy, Missy was a Roman Catholic.

Missy's father had been an Irish gardener who deserted his wife and five children in Somerville, Massachusetts. Missy's mother had to take in Harvard students as boarders to make ends meet. Like both Eleanor and Lucy, Missy had a drinking, often absent, father. All three women would long for their fathers all of their lives. Roosevelt was seventeen years Missy's senior and often signed "Father" on his notes to her. James wrote, "Father, I think, thought of Missy as another of his children."

Lucy had been a threat, but Missy was no hazard to Eleanor or to Lucy despite that Laura "Polly" Delano, Roosevelt's cousin, stated, "Missy was the only woman Franklin ever loved, *everybody* knows that."

Franklin called and invited Lucy to view his triumph, to hear her laughingly call him "Mr. President." Missy provided her with a ticket to the inauguration and arranged for the White House limousine to pick her up at her sister's home on Q Street. Missy and Lucy always treated each other with warmth and respect for both women loved the same man and wanted him to be happy.

While Franklin could not see Lucy on inauguration day, he knew she was there. From a distance on that brisk March day, she heard the Marine Band play "Hail to the Chief." She saw Roosevelt take the oath of office and listened to his brief inaugural address where he assured the American public, "This great nation will endure as it has endured, will revive and will prosper . . . the only thing we have to fear is fear itself."

Despite Roosevelt's monumental accomplishment of becoming the thirty-second president of the United States, 1932 and the beginning of 1933 were difficult times for both Lucy and FDR. In January of 1932 their old friend Livingston Davis committed suicide by shooting himself in the head. In Aiken, Livy would visit Lucy and keep her apprised of what Franklin was doing. He served the same purpose for Roosevelt telling him of Lucy's life. It seemed that the party life Davis maintained, and of which Eleanor disapproved and Lucy and Franklin worried about, had gotten the best of him. Franklin wrote a mutual friend, "Livy's death certainly was a great shock, and I shall miss him dreadfully. I cannot understand it." Livy left his old friend one thousand dollars "in grateful remembrance of joyful comradeship."

Lucy's nephew, Carroll, the twelve-year-old son of her sister Violetta had died of leukemia just prior to Roosevelt's inauguration. It was the Marburys' desire that they bury their son, Carroll Mercer's namesake, in Arlington in his grandfather's grave. When Arlington officials refused their request because the cemetery was becoming too crowded to bury all the family members of a veteran, Lucy contacted FDR. The young Carroll was laid to rest with the grandfather he had never known.

In mid-February of 1933, Italian immigrant Giuseppe "Joseph" Zangara fired five shots at Roosevelt as he finished a brief speech in a Miami park. Zangara was a short man who had to climb on to a chair or bench, accounts vary, to fire at Roosevelt. Seated in his car, Roosevelt was not hurt, but Mayor Anton Cermak of Chicago was wounded as were four others in the crowd. Roosevelt ordered the Secret Service to rush Cermak to the hospital, but the mayor died of his wounds a few weeks later. Zangara who said he hated presidents and the rich, and had also contemplated killing Hoover, was tried, convicted, and executed by electric chair on March 20, 1933.

Both Lucy and Franklin had faced great personal obstacles in the early 1930s to find a measure of peace, despite that it seemed that sometimes illness and death hung over them, but there was more to come. On January 30, 1933, Adolf Hitler had become Chancellor of the Weimar Republic of Germany.

CHAPTER 10

"Bless you as ever. L"

By 1937, Lucy had been married to Winthrop Rutherfurd for seventeen years. The once vibrant sportsman and golf enthusiast was now seventy-five years old and in declining health. While he had a private nurse, he required Lucy's constant care, and she gladly gave it. No one doubted that she adored her husband and enjoyed being with him. She had even accompanied him to prizefights when they had stayed at their pied-a-terre in New York in better days when he was in better health. It was just something ladies didn't do, but if Winty wanted her at his side she obliged, no matter what the situation. Now in failing health, he needed her more than ever.

The Rutherfurd children had thrived under Lucy's care. The four boys, Winthrop, Jr., John, Hugo, and Guy excelled in golf, tennis, and scull racing. In a family where all the men grew over six feet tall, John measured six foot nine. He was also a Golden Gloves champion. At Princeton, he fought and defeated a heavyweight fighter. The press had a heyday reporting on the Ivy Leaguer fighting a street tough.

Alice and Barbara were part of the white dress, debutante scene of Aiken. They competed in and won local horse shows. While Lucy and Winty preferred to stay at home, they did frequent some of the social season activities: golf tournaments, society balls, charity events, races, steeplechase and flat, as well as the various breakfasts, lunches, teas, and dinners that accompanied these events. With Winty's poor health and as the Rutherfurd children grew up, these activities were becoming part of Lucy's past.

Although Barbara had a full-time nurse and governess until she was seventeen, in 1927 at the age of fourteen, she was attending Aiken's exclusive Fermata School for Girls. Marie Eustis Hofmann, the wife of the renowned pianist Josef Hofmann, founded Fermata to educate the resident young ladies of the Winter Colony. The name of the school came from the musical term "fermata" meaning stop or rest. Naturally, the school emphasized music education and appreciation but also stressed equestrian sports, tennis, and golf.* An annual event for the horse-minded community was letting the several hundred students of Aiken Preparatory School and Fermata, mounted on their own ponies, watch the Aiken Steeplechase.

Around this time, Lucy gained the friendship of the artist Elizabeth Shoumatoff who often did portraits of the prominent winter residents of Aiken. Shoumatoff had heard the rumors in the community about FDR and Lucy. Not surprisingly, even one of Lucy's stepchildren once asked, "Lucy, I have just heard that Franklin Roosevelt was in love with you. Was that true, Lucy?" Lucy naturally downplayed the question. The number one rule in the Rutherfurd home was to never mention the

*Fire destroyed the main building in the 1940s. The gymnasium today houses the Fermata Club, which supports swimming and tennis activities.

name of Franklin Delano Roosevelt for several reasons. Besides the obvious, Rutherfurd was a Republican. To those in wealthier circles, Roosevelt was "that man." One of the most loved men in American history was also one of the most hated. Roosevelt's legislation, which forever brought the federal government increasingly into the everyday life of Americans with such programs as Social Security, did not sit well with Republicans who favored little government interference. Abandoning the gold standard and thus devaluing the dollar had affected the worth of the wealthy. Protecting labor unions fostered their growth, not a popular move with large business owners and manufacturers. Congress defeated Roosevelt's 1937 plan to increase the number of Supreme Court justices from nine to twelve. Roosevelt wanted to appoint three more judges because the conservative court opposed much of his New Deal legislation. In May of 1935 the Court had unanimously struck down the NRA, the National Recovery Act, because of federal interference in interstate commerce. As Roosevelt went on to win an unprecedented four terms as president, many feared he would become an autocrat.

In a measure of her stature as a society portrait painter, Elizabeth Shoumatoff stayed at the Willcox Inn when she was in Aiken. The Inn had been the place for America's elite to reside since 1898. Legend had it that the doorman sized up the guests by their shoes. If guests were not shod in expensively made English shoes, there was no room at the inn.

Alice Rutherfurd commissioned Shoumatoff to do a portrait of her stepmother. Alice spoke so lovingly of Lucy that Shoumatoff didn't realize until later that Lucy was not her biological mother. Shoumatoff observed, "All five stepchildren were truly devoted to her." "I can say truly I have seldom seen a mother more beloved and respected than was Lucy by her stepchildren."

As everyone who met Lucy, Shoumatoff was impressed. She found her tall, "lovely and gracious. . . ." as well as "gentle and kindly, interested in others." Her artist's eye discerned that Lucy wore clothes, long flowing tea gowns, to make her look older, in an effort to minimize the great age difference between her and her husband.

Lucy deferred her portrait sitting to have her husband painted first. Shoumatoff described Rutherfurd as handsome and aristocratic. She also thought he somewhat resembled Roosevelt and stated, "Lucy, at one time, admitted this herself." Rutherfurd liked Shoumatoff's work and wanted her to do another painting of him, this one to be done at Allamuchy with his prize terriers. When Shoumatoff came to paint the fox terriers, she found it challenging because of Winty's insistence on having the dogs portrayed accurately in all their show ring glory. Lucy simply wanted a painting of her husband and his dogs. Shoumatoff observed Lucy and Winty's relationship closely and wrote,

> He was the object of constant care and attention. The devotion that Lucy showed him every minute was one of the outstanding features of their life. Everything whirled around him; their life was governed by his invalid regime. She never went out in the evenings and completely devoted her existence to making him happy and comfortable.

For Shoumatoff, Lucy's ". . . mind was constantly preoccupied with her husband's welfare." While acknowledging Lucy's devotion, Shoumatoff had heard the gossip in Aiken, and she couldn't help but ask about President Roosevelt, "You know him?" Lucy responded, "Oh, very well." Shoumatoff noted that Lucy always spoke of the one known in Aiken as "that man" in "admiring terms."

Despite the care lavished on her husband, Lucy could not halt the ravages of time on his body. Yet, Winty's incapacity gave her a measure of freedom to communicate with Franklin by letters and telephone. The old friends often spoke to each other in French, so telephone operators at the White House or in Aiken could not understand their conversations. Lucy's French was excellent as both her personal maid and Barbara's governess were French. Roosevelt's French was adequate. Missy LeHand and Grace Tully, Roosevelt's other secretary, left special instructions with the chief White House switchboard operator, Miss Louise Hackmeister. Roosevelt praised "Hacky" for her ability to find anyone in the world, anywhere, at any time. Her orders were that when Mrs. Rutherfurd called, she must always be put straight through to "the Boss."

A letter from Lucy to FDR survives from 1940 showing her worry over the coming war, "Day by day the news becomes increasingly ominous. . ."* Yet her love and admiration for the man she once hoped to marry remain. She wants to help him if she can, for she recognizes the privileged closed society in which she lives.

> Living—as we do here—in a community of pleasure seekers—who cannot see further than the gloves in their hands—one is terrified by the lack of vision—or understanding of what is going on in the world —

She names several of the Aiken colony who are industrialists and have defense orders and she offers, "If you care to know about his loyalty I can easily find out." Some she trusts for having "sympathy with the administration and backing up of its foreign policy." Some she doesn't.

She recognizes, "This kind of letter is best unwritten and unmailed—and poor darling—to give you one more thing to read or think about is practically criminal." But she goes on mention

*Hitler invaded Poland on September 1, 1939. Great Britain and France declared war on Germany on September 3. On September 5, the United States declared itself neutral.

a personal favor, she wishes "to ask your advice about my youngest step-son [Guy]. . . ." After his law studies she wonders if he should go to work in Washington or to work for his cousin in estate law in New York. Yet war is not far from her mind when she remarks that another stepson should have written to thank Roosevelt "about his company." "Of course, the war may change everything for these boys—and making plans ahead these days makes very little sense." Then after she states, "Bless you as ever, L," she adds an extended postscript:

> Newspapers arrive a day late here—which is trying, and radio reception the worst in the world—which is even more trying. I suppose now more than ever one must live each day as it comes—but it helps to have a milestone in site—and if we have to re-live in a horse and buggy era—it would break my heart—If only it will be a friendly world—a small house would be a joy and one could grow vegetables as well as flowers—

Her love for him had not diminished.

> I know one should be proud—very very proud of your greatness—instead of wishing for the soft life of joy and the world shut out. One is proud and thankful for what you have given to the world and realizes how much more must still be given this greedy world—which never asks in vain—You have breathed new life into its spirit—and the fate of all that is good is in your dear blessed and capable hands.

She closes her letter, "As always L."

* * *

After his continuous decline of 1937, Winthrop Rutherfurd suffered a stroke in early spring 1941. By June he had a second stroke. He could barely use his right arm. The man who once commanded any room he entered, just as Lucy turned heads in any room she entered, now had difficulty speaking. Lucy wanted to bring him to Washington to see a specialist. She contacted FDR to get Winty into Walter Reed Hospital. Lucy and Franklin's old friend, and Winty's former sister-in-law, Edith Eustis, arranged for Lucy to visit Roosevelt at the White House. For years, it was believed that Lucy did not keep this appointment to see her old flame but sent Alice and Barbara in her place.* The President's official schedule shows on June 5, 1941, "1555–1740: Returned from Office to Study White House accompanied by Mrs. Johnson."** Mrs. Johnson was Lucy's Secret Service code name.

The earlier date of Lucy's visit would be interesting on its own merit, but when coupled with other events, it sheds new light on the dynamic of Franklin Roosevelt and the women who loved him. Preceding his meeting with "Mrs. Johnson," the log notes, "1130: To Marguerite A. LeHand's apartment." Following the departure of Mrs. Johnson at 1740, the log reads, "1740: To Marguerite A. LeHand's apartment." On the evening prior to Lucy's visit to the White House, Missy LeHand had suffered a stroke, and Roosevelt was keeping a close watch on her.

For twenty years Missy had loved her F.D. She had served him, protected him, soothed him through the dark days of polio and the triumph of becoming president. She was the gatekeeper to the Oval Office. She relished her power that supplicants had to get past her to get to him. She advised his staff, cabinet members, members of Congress, even his family "when to approach" the president. She was the one who cried over his welfare when he told the country in 1940 that he would be the first president to run for a third term in 175 years. Now at forty-three Missy was sharing him with other women who threatened her place, and she didn't like it.

---

*Joseph Alsop reports this in his *FDR: A Centenary Remembrance* (p. 72).

**Most historians dated "Mrs. Johnson's" first chronicled visit to the White House as Friday, August 1, 1941. Ellen Feldman verified the earlier date.

Roosevelt had been carrying on a flirtation with Crown Princess Martha of Norway since she had sought asylum in the United States in August 1940. This new attachment and the knowledge that Rutherfurd's infirmary allowed Lucy more freedom may well have concerned Missy. Letters and phone calls between FDR and Lucy would no longer suffice. After the June 5 visit, Lucy could start coming regularly to the White House. Was it the last straw for Missy? As Eleanor well knew when she forbade any contact between her husband and Lucy, who can compete with the one who got away?

Roosevelt first met Princess Martha and her husband, Prince Olav, in the spring of 1939 when they came to the United States to dedicate the Norwegian exhibit at the World's Fair in New York City. Princess Martha was the daughter of a Swedish prince and a Danish princess. Born in 1901, she married Prince Olav, the heir to the throne of Norway, in 1929. They had two princesses, Ragnild and Astrid and a prince, Harald.* The Nazis invaded Norway early in April 1940, and King Haakon refused to surrender. He fled, along with members of the royal family and the Parliament, into the north. When the Nazis closed in, he and his son, Olav, fled to London to run the Norwegian government in exile. Princess Martha, for she feared the Nazis wanted to kidnap her children, accepted asylum from Roosevelt.

Roosevelt once said, "Nothing is more pleasing to the eye than a good-looking lady, nothing more refreshing to the spirit than the company of one, nothing more flattering to the ego than the affection of one." Just as for Lucy and Missy, now for Princess Martha, FDR could do no wrong. She sat by him, hung on his words, and looked into his eyes with admiration and love. She was "pleasing to the eye" for she looked "exactly as a princess should. . . ."

---

*Prince Olav succeeded to the throne in 1957. Prince Harald succeeded his father in 1992 and reigns today as King Harald V. Princess Martha died in 1954.

Statuesque, her brown eyes, creamy complexion, and good bone structure attested to her aristocratic breeding. Despite the hardships she had endured, she still laughed and had a good time.

She and her children, her lady-in-waiting, court chamberlain, and servants first visited Hyde Park in September. They attended a Sunday morning service on September 8 at St. James Episcopal Church, the Roosevelt family church, as part of a national day of prayer declared by the president. Germany's "blitz" or relentless bombing of London had begun the night before. The United States seemed daily to march progressively toward war. After the service, Sara Roosevelt hosted a lunch at Springhill. Joining Princess Martha and her retinue were the former empress of the Austro-Hungarian Empire, Zita, and her two sons who also had sanctuary in the United States. Sara who didn't feel "anyone was her social equal, except maybe the queen of England, and she wasn't sure about that," was in her element presiding over a luncheon table of exiled royals.

After the Hyde Park stay, Roosevelt issued an invitation for Martha and her entourage to stay at the White House. They took up residence in the Rose Suite on the second floor of the White House while they searched, with the help of Roosevelt, for a proper residence. She became part of Roosevelt's White House life, sharing tea with him in the afternoon, joining in the "children's hour" cocktails, and motoring around the countryside with him. Even after her family found an estate, Pook's Hill in Bethesda, Maryland, she still regularly visited the White House, and Roosevelt drove out to visit her. Because he greeted her and left her with a kiss, the White House staff came to call her "the president's girlfriend."

After thirty years, Eleanor was still "the" wife, and she had seen all this before. "There was always a Martha for relaxation and for the non-ending pleasure of having an admiring audience for every breath," she remarked to her friend Joseph Lash. Missy LeHand, the "other" wife, who for twenty years was the one who went over his stamp collection with him, sat by him in his automobile or on his houseboat, and worked alongside him, did not take his attentions toward Martha so nonchalantly.

In the spring of 1941 Missy was not sleeping well. As the war in Europe advanced, Roosevelt worked longer hours into the night with Missy always at his side. In addition to her secretarial duties and running the household for Eleanor, she often had to change into evening attire at a moment's notice to act as the president's hostess as Franklin more and more needed Eleanor to travel for him. The job was overwhelming Missy and her heart had been damaged by rheumatic fever. Others noticed that the usual easygoing woman was now subject to flares of temper.

In June of 1927, she had collapsed at Warm Springs. It was a harbinger of things to come. Physicians first thought she had had a mild heart attack because of her weakened heart, but she was also depressed and sometimes delirious. For Grace Tully, it was "a little crackup." Missy's friend Barbara Curtis was not so diplomatic; she called it "a nervous breakdown." The cause of her breakdown? Certainly overwork, but that spring Roosevelt had sold the houseboat, the *Larooco*. For three years from 1924 until 1927, Missy had cruised with FDR on that boat in the winter and then they would move on to Warm Springs for his therapy. Now as Roosevelt was considering running for governor, Missy sensed her relationship with Roosevelt was changing. She did not want him to run for governor, "Don't you dare. Don't you dare," she repeatedly told him.

When Roosevelt decided to enter the race, Missy suffered another breakdown. By the time the election was over and the Roosevelts moved into the governor's mansion, Missy had recovered and went with them. With Eleanor's blessing, Missy had her own bedroom on the second floor next to FDR's.

The White House staff held an annual party hosted by Harry Sommerville, the manager of Washington, D.C.'s Willard Hotel. The Willard Hotel, just a few blocks from the White House, had been an inn since 1847 and boasted that every president since Zachary Taylor had lodged there.* While the staff usually partied at the famous hotel, on June 4, 1941, Mr. Somerville hosted the dinner at the White House so Roosevelt could attend. Present were Missy, her helper Grace Tully, and other members of FDR's staff. When Missy told Grace Tully she was tired, Tully urged her to go to her room, but Missy felt it violated protocol to leave before Roosevelt departed. He had barely left the room at 9:30 when Missy screamed and collapsed. The president's doctor, Ross McIntire, and his physical therapist, George Fox, took her to her room and sedated her.

When Eleanor heard of Missy's illness, she asked Maggie Parks, a retired servant Missy liked, to return and care for her. Maggie listened to her ramblings that her work was piling up and the president would be unhappy. She heard her call out for her "F.D." Maggie's diagnosis, she shared with her daughter, was that "the strain of loving and knowing nothing can come of it" had caused Missy's collapse.

Two weeks later, on June 21, she had a major stroke that took her to Doctor's Hospital. Like Rutherfurd the stroke caused her to lose the use of her right arm and leg and to speak incoherently, only Rutherfurd was seventy-nine and Missy forty-three.

Missy refused all visitors except the Roosevelts. Despite his own infirmaries and life-and-death physical struggles, FDR had trained himself to disregard misery. He smiled and laughed when he saw her and told her cheery anecdotes of White House happenings. Missy often could do no more than cry. He could do no more than leave. Unable to voice his despair, he paid her medical expenses, ensuring her round-the-clock medical care. The strain of Missy's infirmity sent FDR to bed. Eleanor wrote her daughter, "Missy has

---

*The Willard had other famous guests: Buffalo Bill, Charles Dickens, P. T. Barnum, and Mark Twain to name a few. It is still an elegant hotel today. "What this country needs is a good 5-cent cigar," Thomas R. Marshall, Woodrow Wilson's vice president, mouthed in response to the Willard's prices.

been worse for the last few days and that may be at the bottom of much of Pa's trouble."

Eleanor handled Missy's disability better. She visited her often, bringing gifts and notes from well-wishers. For Elliott Roosevelt, "Mother was more protective and upset about Missy's illness than Father. He seemed to accept it and go through the loss without its affecting him nearly as much as I would have thought it would have affected him." James recognized that Missy's absence was felt deeply by his father. "He missed Missy in a very practical way but even more than most men might miss their secretaries. Physically, he could not do for himself what most men could do, and she had seen to his needs."

After she left the hospital, Roosevelt sent her to Warm Springs to recuperate. She would eventually live out her days at home north of Boston. With physical therapy, Missy improved a little over time. She did learn to walk again with a heavy brace and crutches like her beloved F.D. She understood what others said, but she could only speak a few phrases. It was clear she would not return to work at the White House. Roosevelt recognized her loyalty, for he told his son James, "She served me so well for so long and asked so little in return." In November after her stroke, Roosevelt rewrote his will dividing his estate between Eleanor and Missy, about 1.5 million dollars each. Missy's share was to cover "all expenses for medical attention, care and treatment during her lifetime." If she preceded him in death, all would go to Eleanor. Missy died on July 31, 1944, at the age of forty-six. Roosevelt did not change his will as he told James, "Missy didn't make it, her half already has reverted to mother, and so the clause is inoperative. I don't have to change it, so I won't." He also remarked to his son about leaving money to Missy for her medical expenses, "Some may try to make something of that. They shouldn't, but they will. If it embarrasses mother, I'm sorry. It shouldn't, but it may."

CHAPTER 11

"Your dear blessed and capable hands"

The New England, Quaker poet John Greenleaf Whittier wrote *Maud Muller* in 1867. It contains lines that tug at the heart of any human being with any regrets, "For of all sad words of tongue and pen, the saddest are these: 'It might have been.'" FDR and Lucy must have had similar sentiments when they met for the first time in over twenty years on June 5, 1941. At their respective ages of fifty-nine and fifty, their world was a very different place than when they had parted in 1918. When Roosevelt was last with Lucy, he had been a vigorous man on the verge of a career in public service. Lucy had been a beautiful young woman who had not yet discovered her life's purpose. Now Roosevelt was at the pinnacle of American political life, and Lucy had found love and fulfillment in a large family. They had said good-bye at the end of the "war to end all wars," and now the United States seemed destined to enter World War II.

When Great Britain and France declared war against Germany on September 3, 1939, Roosevelt in one of his fireside chats to the American people stated the United States would try to stay out of the war, but he knew he could not "ask that every American remain neutral in thought." By the spring of 1940, Hitler's blitzkrieg or lightning war had defeated nearly every western European nation. When France fell in May, only England stood against Germany. The blitz, Germany's relentless bombing of England, did not destroy the Royal Air Force, let alone the fortitude of the English people. As a result Hitler abandoned his idea to invade England in 1940. It was on this occasion that the new Prime Minister, Winston Churchill, declared of the Battle of Britain, "Never in the field of human conflict was so much owed by so many to so few." Churchill had replaced Neville Chamberlain in the spring of 1940 as the British turned against the idea of appeasing Hitler. Chamberlain had returned from his meeting with Hitler in Munich on the future of Czechoslovakia in 1938 stating that there would be "peace in our time." He then advised his fellow citizens, "Go home and get a nice quiet sleep."

From the beginning, many Americans, who still had memories of World War I, did not want to get involved in yet another European conflict. Americans favored isolationism even though Italy had conquered Ethiopia and aligned itself with Germany, and Japan had invaded China in July 1937. In 1940 the Democratic Party nominated Roosevelt for an historic third term against the Republican candidate Wendell Willkie. The campaign centered on America's role in the hostilities. While Willkie was no isolationist, he charged that Roosevelt would lead the country into warfare. Roosevelt promised that the United States would stay out of the war, and in the end, the American voters still trusted FDR's leadership.

After the election, Roosevelt delivered his State of the Union address on January 6, 1941, to the Seventy-Seventh Congress. He proposed the Lend Lease program to supply Great Britain with weapons and war supplies even if they no longer had the money to buy them. The United States would "lend" materials to Britain or any nation aligned with the United States. In addition, he called for "a swift and driving increase in our armament production." He concluded his speech by declaring, "In the future days which we seek to secure, we look forward to a world founded upon four essential human freedoms." The *Saturday Evening Post*'s Norman Rockwell later celebrated those four freedoms in paintings that came to adorn many American homes—freedom of speech, freedom of worship, freedom from want, and freedom from fear.

With both Missy LeHand and Winthrop Rutherfurd incapacitated and Eleanor Roosevelt preoccupied with her own causes and her traveling, it was easier for Franklin and Lucy to meet. The White House usher's diary records that on August 1, 1941, Mrs. Paul Johnson visited the president at 8:40 that evening. They spent the evening alone, and she left at 11:00. She returned for dinner the following evening departing at midnight. Eleanor was away at Campobello. On November 9, Mrs. Johnson and her daughter had tea with the president, and then Mrs. Johnson had dinner with Roosevelt in his study the same evening; they dined alone. Eleanor was in New York. Barbara had dinner in Roosevelt's study with him and Harry Hopkins, the secretary of commerce, in December. In the spring of 1942, Mrs. Johnson had dinner twice at the White House. In October, as Eleanor journeyed to England, she ate dinner with Franklin and took tea with him the subsequent afternoon. On these occasions, Roosevelt sent a car to pick Lucy up at her sister's home on Q Street in Washington and bring her to him.

With increased personal contact, Lucy began to request things of the president for her family and friends. After returning from her June 5 visit, Lucy received requested information from FDR on getting her stepson John into the Supply Corps Reserve. Roosevelt noted that while the corps had reached its quota, they still needed people with accounting experience. Fortunately, John was a CPA.

The commander in chief could ensure room for another ensign. On June 23, 1941, John wrote to thank the president, "It was awfully nice of you to see me in Washington, and Mother and I especially enjoyed your notation . . . about my case." In July 19, 1942, John wrote Roosevelt from Seattle thanking him again for the opportunity to serve. The next day the President responded, "I hear from your Mother that your family has joined you."

On March 18, 1942, Lucy writes FDR about her friend Mrs. Hare Lippincott. Can she get her fifteen-year-old grandson on a ship to England to get back to his family and to join the Royal Navy when he turns sixteen? Roosevelt responds to Mrs. Lippincott a week later that he can find a space for her grandson in May or June to travel to London to see his mother and his father, in diplomatic service.

Between Lucy's increasing visits to the White House, Roosevelt called upon her at Violetta's home when she was in town. Two unmarked automobiles would pull up in front of the Marbury home. One car held the president, the other the Secret Service. A Secret Service agent would come to the door for Mrs. Johnson. The maid knew who was asking for Mrs. Johnson but in her loyalty never revealed the secret. The agent would escort Lucy out to the President's car. Other times they would meet on a road outside Georgetown. Lucy would be waiting for Franklin in a car as the Secret Service drove the president to their rendezvous.

FDR and Lucy sat together alone in the backseat of the unmarked presidential automobile separated from the driver by a glass partition. He drove the old friends around Washington, through Rock Creek Park, and into Virginia and Maryland along the same roads they had traveled so many years ago. No record exists of their conversations, but it is not difficult to speculate what they said to each other.

The reunion of FDR and his Lucy would be the highlight of 1941 for both of them. In addition to the illnesses of Missy and

Winty, Sara Roosevelt was in her decline. In June she had suffered a stroke at Campobello and, as a proud woman, preferred to stay in her room. She refused a nurse until her son insisted for his own "peace of mind." When she returned to her Hyde Park home in early September, she was weak and had difficulty breathing. Her condition so alarmed Eleanor that she insisted Franklin come home to Springwood. While Sara planned to be "downstairs on the porch" to meet her son, she could not get out of bed. The best she could do was to dress up in an expensive bed jacket for his arrival on September 6. "When my son comes and sits there beside me with the smile that is *not* reserved for the voters, I just look at his face and think that it has everything—wisdom and goodness and sweetness."

He spent the day talking with his mother, telling her of Washington events and of his recent meeting with Churchill, the first time the two had met as leaders. Their discussions had taken place at sea with Roosevelt arriving on the *Augusta* and Churchill on the *Prince of Wales*. At the Atlantic Conference, as the meeting became known, the two allies discussed Japan's growing aggression in the Pacific and the peace plans for after the Nazis were defeated.*

Her son's visit cheered her up, and the family hoped she had rallied, but that evening she slipped into unconsciousness. With the son she had adored and enshrined in her home in countless photographs and paintings by her bedside, she died a little after noon the next day. In two weeks she would have been eighty-seven. "Mrs. James" had outlived her husband by forty-one years. At her death, the largest oak tree on her estate came crashing to the ground. While the true cause was the thin soil over base rock in Dutchess County, Roosevelt's bodyguard Mike Reilly noted that the president was "struck, as we all were, by the obvious symbolism."

---

*Harry Hopkins feared such two strong egos, both used to all the attention, might clash. He didn't need to worry. They became good friends.

Eleanor's emotions were compounded by the illness of her younger brother Hall who had collapsed the night of Sara's death. Years of drinking had destroyed his liver, and he died at the age of forty-nine three weeks later. "The loss of a brother is always a sad breaking of a family tie," but for her, she wrote, it was more, "like losing a child." Conflicted by sentiments toward the mother-in-law who had ruled her early years as a young wife, Eleanor attended to the details of the funeral.

> I looked at my mother-in-law's face after she was dead & I understood so many things I had never seen before. It is dreadful to have lived so close to someone for 36 years & to feel no deep affection or sense of loss. It's hard on Franklin, & the material details are appalling & there of course I can be of some use.

Roosevelt, so devoted to his mother, wore a mourning band on his arm for over a year, but he kept the depth of his grief hidden from those around him. Following her funeral, he and Grace Tully were going through his mother's belongings when they came across a box that contained particularly personal items: locks of her son's hair, his christening dress, his baby shoes, letters he had written her. Tears filled the president's eyes, and Miss Tully left him alone as he wished. Neither she, nor any of his staff, had ever seen him cry.

Lucy's own mother, the formidable Minna Mercer, as she now preferred to be called, had gone into the Waverly Sanitarium in Rockville, Maryland, in February of 1941. At the age of seventy-seven, she had entered the sanitarium twelve miles from Washington because of her "heart high blood pressure." Prior to her poor health, she had been living at the Wyoming Apartments. Her age brought further eccentricity. She seldom went out preferring to stay at home and read. Her family found that when they went to visit her, she never asked them to sit, let alone offered them any refreshment, so they stood awkwardly in front of her. She lived on her husband's military pension, and taxed her daughters' generosity by her inclination to buy flowers and books rather than food. She spent much of her time writing the Veteran's Bureau asking for more funds or trying to find her checks. Her propensity to move from hotels to apartments caused the Director of Finance at one point to write and declare that she would receive no more checks until she had a permanent address on file.

On November 28, 1941, Roosevelt left Washington to attend the annual Thanksgiving dinner of the polio patients at Warm Springs, Georgia. He and Grace Tully went to visit Missy LeHand who was undergoing physical therapy there in a private cottage with a private nurse. She could still not speak beyond a few words. The president was tired and worried about the worsening state of affairs with Japan. After fifteen minutes with Missy, he left.

His Secretary of State, Cordell Hull, certain an attack would come soon, phoned Roosevelt, and FDR agreed to return to Washington the next day. During the week of December 1, the United States negotiated with the Japanese in an effort to avert war. The Japanese offered to withdraw from Indochina if the United States would resume trade with them, particularly selling them oil. Hull would not consider the proposal until the Japanese stopped the occupation of China. Negotiations had hit a brick wall. War seemed inevitable. By December 6, intelligence officials had deciphered a coded message from Tokyo to the Japanese ambassador to the United States. All of Hull's proposals for peace were to be rejected.

The first of three waves of Japanese planes bombed the American fleet at Pearl Harbor just after 7:30 A.M., local time. Fortunately, half the fleet, which included three aircraft carriers, was not there. In just over two hours, 188 airplanes, eight battleships including the *Arizona*, three light cruisers, three destroyers, and nearly thirty five hundred people were gone. Secretary of the Navy Frank Knox called the president at 1:30 P.M. local time and thus the news began to spread across the land. By 5:00 P.M. Roosevelt called Grace Tully into his study. He spoke calmly to his secretary, "Sit down, Grace. I'm going before Congress tomorrow. I'd like to dictate my message. It will be short."

> Yesterday comma December 7 comma 1941 dash a day which will live in infamy dash the United States of America was suddenly and deliberately attacked by naval and air forces of the Empire of Japan period paragraph.

The date cemented a generation to the question, "Where were you?"

All who saw Roosevelt that day remarked on his stoicism. Eleanor recalled that he was "very strained and tired. But he was completely calm. His reaction to any great event was always to be calm. If it was something that went bad, he just became almost like an iceberg, and there was never the slightest emotion that was allowed to show."

What Lucy had written FDR when she sensed the coming war, was now prophetic: "the fate of all that is good is in your dear blessed and capable hands."

CHAPTER 12

"I am alone"

Upon hearing of the attack on Pearl Harbor, Winston Churchill remarked, "To have the United States at our side was to me the greatest joy. Now at this very moment I knew the United States was in the war, up to the neck and in to the death."

Within days of the Pearl Harbor attack, Germany and Italy declared war on the United States. Isolationism was dead; patriotism was the order of the day. The song "Remember Pearl Harbor" written by Don Reid, music by Reid and Sammy Kaye, became an instant hit. Americans flew flags, planted victory gardens, collected scrap metal for the war effort, and endured rationing of gasoline, food, and other commodities destined for the military. Local civil defense wardens urged fellow citizens to look for enemy submarines along the coasts and planes in the sky. People hung blackout curtains in their homes, no more fireplace smoke or streetlights after dark. They abided by slogans they saw everywhere, "Buy War Bonds!" and "Loose Lips Sink Ships."

The war put great demands on the populace, the military, and the economy. By the time the war was over twelve million people had entered the armed forces and fifteen million left their home towns, 20 percent of the population, to work in factories and shipyards for the war effort. Six million women entered the work force to fill the jobs vacated by men who'd gone off to war. These women made the planes and ships for America to fight the war. They were immortalized in Rosie the Riveter posters. Portrayed in overalls, scarf on her head, with goggles, Rosie is a proud worker. The posters celebrated her power with such phrases as "She's a WOW Woman!" (Woman Ordinance Worker) or "We Can Do It." Often a soldier was in the background of the poster as it intoned, "She Backs Our Boys."*

As the citizens of the United States mobilized for war so did the Roosevelt and Rutherfurd families. James Roosevelt wrote that "By December 7, 1941, all FDR's sons, were in the service, either in the active reserve or on active duty. Franklin was in the naval reserve, John had been commissioned an ensign in the navy early in the year, Elliott was in the army air force and I was in the marines." Lucy's contact with the president extended to her children. Roosevelt would telegram Barbara yearly on her birthday signing it "Godfather." Just before the Allies invaded Sicily in July of 1943, he wires her at Allamuchy, "It is today even more essential that you stop in Washington to visit your Godfather." A week after D-Day, the invasion of Normandy on June 6, 1944, his telegram reaches her in Aiken. "Thinking of you today. Hope you will come up and see me soon." The man who held the destiny of the free world in his hands did not forget the birthday of his beloved friend's daughter.

---

*Rosie still commands respect. Norman Rockwell's painting of her for the May 29, 1943, cover of *The Saturday Evening Post* sold at Southeby's in May 2002 for nearly five million dollars.

The youngest Rutherfurd boy, Guy, had consulted with Roosevelt, per Lucy's request, on his career plans. He had finished his law degree at the University of Virginia where Franklin, Jr. was also studying. At Roosevelt's recommendation, he had taken the New York bar exam before enlisting. By June 25, 1942, Guy was writing the president and thanking him for his help in getting into the navy. Commissioned as an ensign in the naval reserve, he was serving in Newport, Rhode Island. The White House Visitor's Book records a visit from Winthrop, Jr. on June 26, 1941, and three off the record visits from him in 1943. In May he was a lieutenant, in July and September he was listed as a captain. In the spring of 1943, Hugo contacted the president asking him to intervene and help him get active sea duty. Roosevelt put him in touch with Vice Admiral Ross McIntire, his personal physician and navy admiral.

Early in 1943, Roosevelt phoned his daughter, Anna, in Seattle and asked her to "be nice" to John Rutherfurd who was there on temporary duty.* Anna recalled not thinking too much about it "because Father often called with the same request about other people—including the then Crown Prince and Princess of Norway and Lord and Lady Halifax . . . (he was then British Ambassador to the United States)." She did recognize that he must be "a stepson of Lucy Mercer Rutherfurd's."

Roosevelt had also supplied John Rutherfurd and his wife with two of his last four tickets to attend Churchill's second address to a joint session of Congress on May 19, 1943. Usually, Eleanor dispensed the tickets for the presidential box, but on this occasion, FDR requested seven tickets that he wanted to distribute. Grace Tully handed out the tickets per the president's

*Anna and Curtis Dall had divorced. She married John Boettiger and moved to Seattle where he worked on the *Seattle Post-Intelligencer*. They divorced in 1949. She married James Halsted in 1952.

wishes. In addition to the Rutherfurds, tickets went to the British Minister of Transport, Lord Leathers, and to the Ambassador to the Vatican and his wife, Mr. and Mrs. Myron Taylor. The Duke and Duchess of Windsor received Roosevelt's last two tickets.

All assembled heard Churchill describe the war effort, "For more than five hundred days—every day a day we have toiled and suffered and dared, shoulder to shoulder against the cruel enemy—we have acted in close combination or concert in many parts of the world, on land, on sea, and in the air."

Eleanor, unaware of the increasing friendliness of Lucy and her family with the president in her absence, had not forgotten the hurt caused by her former social secretary and her husband. In 1943, she wrote her friend Joseph P. Lash about the effect of Lucy Mercer on her life. "There was a war then too & the bottom dropped out of my own particular world & I faced myself, my surroundings, my world, honestly for the first time. I really grew up that year. . . ."

Eleanor had first met Lash in 1939 when he was a member of the American Student Union who favored political upheaval in American social and economic order. He had once been a member of the Socialist Party and had traveled to Spain but saw no action in the Spanish Civil War. When he appeared before the House Un-American Activities Committee, Eleanor invited him and some of his friends back to the White House. From the beginning of their relationship, she opened up to the young man because she identified with his passion for causes and as Lash recounted, "my miseries reminded her of her own when she was young. Insecurity, shyness, lack of social grace, she had had to conquer them all and helping someone she cared about do the same filled a deep unquenchable longing to feel needed and useful." Lash went on to write six books about the Roosevelts because of his close friendship with Eleanor.

It was at her home, Val-Kill, where Eleanor had long talks with two of her closest friends, Joseph Lash and Lorena Hickok, about Lucy and other events in her life. At Val-Kill she felt liberated. It was the only home she called her own. She had grown up in her grandmother's mansion. When she married, her mother-in-law had built and furnished a townhouse for the newlyweds in New York City. The vacation home at Campobello, the mansion at Hyde Park, these were Roosevelt domiciles.

In August 1924 she had picnicked at Hyde Park with FDR and friends from the New York Democratic Committee, Nancy Cook and Marion Dickerman. As Eleanor bemoaned their last outing because Sara closed the big house in the fall, Franklin offered the three women some acreage from the Roosevelt estate to build a cottage where they could enjoy the Hudson River countryside year round. Roosevelt worked with the architect Henry Toombs to design the modest home in Dutch colonial style named Val-Kill after a nearby stream. By 1925, Nan and Marion were living in the cottage, and they stayed there until 1947. At last, Eleanor had a place where she wasn't under her mother-in-law's rules. As first lady it became her refuge. She spent weekends and holidays there with friends or often alone to recover from her constant travels around the nation.*

The three women along with another friend, Catherine O'Day, started a business at Val-Kill in 1926. They built a factory to employ rural Dutchess County farm workers so they wouldn't leave to find employment in the city. The factory, which turned out replicas of early American furniture, rugs, and dishes, lasted

---

*Eleanor's simple home saw many exalted visitors. When dignitaries such as Churchill or Queen Wilhemina of the Netherlands visited the president at Springhill, they journeyed the few miles for a casual meal at Val-Kill. After Roosevelt's death, Eleanor received many world leaders there: Soviet Premier Khrushchev, Emperor Haile Selassie of Ethiopia, Nehru of India, and John F. Kennedy seeking her support for his 1960 presidential campaign.

for ten years but closed with many other businesses during the Great Depression. Eleanor then converted the factory building into apartments and guest rooms to handle the overflow from the cottage.

A frequent guest of Val-Kill was Lorena Hickok, affectionately known as Hick. The two women became friends in 1932 when Hick was thirty-nine and Eleanor forty-eight. Then Hick was one of the best-known reporters in the country. In an era when few women worked for newspapers, she had been with the Associated Press for twelve years. She covered Eleanor in the 1932 campaign at a time when Eleanor was apprehensive about returning to Washington, and the painful period it represented in her life. In addition, the idea of becoming first lady daunted her. During the campaign, Eleanor and Hick told each other their life stories. Because of her profession, Hick had to be "one of the boys." She smoked cigars, gambled, and liked bourbon. Heavyset, she was most comfortable in trousers and flannel, but dressed professionally with makeup, jewelry, and coifed hair when it was called for. She came from a social spectrum far removed from Eleanor's, for she had grown up on a poor Wisconsin dairy farm with an extremely abusive father who killed her pets when he wasn't beating on her or her mother. Both women understood loneliness and sensed the scars on each other's souls. Eleanor confided in Hick how FDR's affair with Lucy had affected her, how she had had to reinvent herself. Hick told her of working in rooming houses to pay for her education and of the loss of her love, Ellie Morse, a wealthy young woman. She and Ellie had lived together for six years when Ellie left to marry an old boyfriend.

At the top of her career but in love again, Hick abandoned her reporter's impartiality to help Eleanor ease into the role of first lady, to make it her own. She helped Eleanor write magazine articles. When Eleanor sent her pages of details of her workday, Hick encouraged her to turn those letters into her own syndicated column, "My Day." She recommended Eleanor hold her own press conferences. To increase the number of women in the press ranks, the first lady invited only female reporters.

A multitude of letters between Hick and Eleanor attest to their devotion to each other and raise questions of the nature of their relationship. After FDR's first inauguration, she writes Hick, "Oh! I want to put my arms around you. I ache to hold you close. Your ring is a great comfort. I look at it and think she does love me, or I wouldn't be wearing it." While Lucy watched Roosevelt take the oath of office from a distance, Eleanor gazed at a sapphire ring Hick had given her prior to the inauguration.

The daily letters are filled with emotional and physical longing. Hick wants to "kiss the soft spot" of Eleanor's mouth. Eleanor longs to lie down beside her. Lillian Rogers Parks, the White House maid, wrote that the closeness of Hick and Eleanor was "obvious to some servants on the very day of the inaugural ceremonies." Hick was to interview the new first lady, and they conducted the interview in Eleanor's bathroom. Parks thought this, "hardly the kind of thing one would do with an ordinary reporter. Or even with an adult friend."

Eleanor told Lash, "Every woman wants to be first to someone sometime in her life and that desire is the explanation for many strange things women do." We can't know if they expressed their love for each other beyond the kisses and hugs of women friends, and it doesn't matter any more than knowing how intimate Lucy and FDR were. Love is love, and it changes people. For Hick, Eleanor came first, and Eleanor needed love and loyalty from someone during those stressful years when she transformed herself into more than the role of first lady of the United States required. Eleanor recognized this, "You taught me more than you know. . . ." She admitted to Hick, "You've made of me so much more of a person just to be worthy of you."

Hick left the Associated Press in 1933 to be closer to Eleanor. For a while, she worked with Harry Hopkins to evaluate WPA projects but as Eleanor's star rose Hick's began to dim. Once a top reporter with her own money, friends, prestige, she resented being identified as Eleanor's secretary in photographs when her image was even allowed. Often she was trimmed from photographs of family gatherings before they were issued. As Eleanor gained widespread respect and love, she needed Hick less. Hick moved into Louis Howe's old room in the White House in 1941 when she became executive secretary to the Women's Division of the Democratic National Committee and could not afford to rent an apartment. She stayed there for four years not always content with what time Eleanor could spare for her. Hick exclaimed, "I couldn't bear the idea of being in Washington and hardly ever seeing her." Hick died in 1968, six years after her beloved Eleanor.

Eleanor was not the only one who liked a private retreat away from the Roosevelt Hyde Park mansion. Franklin had his own domicile, Top Cottage, which he started to build in 1938 in the hills above the Val-Kill area with a view of the Hudson River Valley and the Catskills. With Henry J. Toombs, who had designed Val-Kill, Roosevelt built the one story house to accommodate his special needs for living in a wheelchair. The stove was low so he could cook scrambled eggs from the wheelchair. No doors had doorsills so he could easily roll from room to room. Here he would write his memoirs when he left office.

Understandably, Sara didn't like it that both her son and daughter-in-law preferred separate homes away from her. When Roosevelt came home to Hyde Park, he always visited his "Dream House" as the press called it, but he had to sleep at Springwood as promised to his mother as long as she was alive. While Sara or Eleanor didn't want to join Franklin at Top Cottage, several others did. Not only Missy but Margaret "Daisy"

Suckley, his sixth cousin and friend, thought she'd share the cottage with FDR when it was completed in 1939. If either woman knew of the other's plans, it isn't known. Perhaps this was another reason Roosevelt chose to run for president again in 1940.

In the spring of 1943, Shoumatoff was again in Aiken visiting Lucy and Winty who was by then a bedridden invalid. As she and Lucy drank tea, Lucy remarked, "You should really paint the president. Would you do a portrait of him if it was arranged?" Shoumatoff reluctantly agreed believing that it would be too difficult to schedule. To her surprise, Lucy called her the next morning at the Willcox Inn to say that she had telephoned the president. He would sit for a portrait in two weeks. Shoumatoff questioned how the president could squeeze in time for sittings in the midst of a war. After all, he had just returned from meeting with Churchill at Casablanca. Lucy responded, "Oh, I told him that he could continue his work while you painted, and that you worked very fast and would not require much of his time. He said he could give you two mornings."

Shoumatoff had difficulty in finding lodging in wartime Washington and prevailed upon her friendship with the Richard Mellons to take her in. They were astonished at the subject of her commission.

When Shoumatoff entered the president's office, he greeted her with a friendliness described by others, as "his hand seems to stretch across the entire room." "How is Mrs. Rutherfurd? And how is Barbara?" he asked. The president wanted a small portrait of ten by twelve. When his gray suit and blue tie seemed too drab for Shoumatoff, Roosevelt recommended his navy cape. When her time ran out the next day, Roosevelt agreed to another half hour to be shaved from his lunch hour. She finished the details with William D. Simmons, Roosevelt's assistant, wearing the president's cape in the Constitution Room. When Shoumatoff presented the finished picture to Lucy in Aiken a few weeks later, she was pleased as was the president who wanted prints for some friends. Roosevelt liked the portrait, and he later invited Shoumatoff and her brother to visit him at Hyde Park.

In March 1944 in Aiken, Winty steadily slipped away from Lucy. Three years after his stroke, he died on the nineteenth. He was eighty-two years old. As he had wished, Lucy returned his body to Tranquility for burial. Now dressed in black, Lucy walked through the rooms of Tranquility. Compared to life in Aiken with neighbors, friends, and a variety of diversions, living at Allamuchy was a lonely existence. The big, isolated house was populated with servants who came and went, as Rutherfurd never tolerated impropriety on their part. He had dismissed a young footman who had swum out to a raft to flirt, in the presence of Barbara, with her pretty, French nurse. Only Lucy's sister, Violetta, and her children visited her at Tranquility. Winty and Lucy had built a stone guesthouse for her sister's summer visits.

In another month, Lucy would turn fifty-three. They had been married twenty-four years. Winty had lived a long, full life. Because of their age differences, Lucy knew her husband would die before her, still she found it hard to say, "I am alone."

CHAPTER 13

"His beloved presence"

In late November 1943, for the first time, the Soviet leader Joseph Stalin would join Churchill and Roosevelt at a summit to be held in Tehran, Iran. There the world leaders would meet to discuss plans for an invasion of Europe from the north, Operation Overlord. Much to the disappointment of Eleanor and Anna, Roosevelt refused to take them with him although he had invited Elliott, FDR, Jr., and Anna's husband, John Boettiger who was stationed in North Africa. "Absolutely no women," declared FDR. The navy would not allow women on shipboard. When photographs were printed of the meeting showing Churchill with his daughter Sarah and Chiang Kai-Shek of China with his wife, Madame Chiang, the angry Eleanor wrote her husband, "I've been amused that Madame Chiang and Sarah Churchill were in the party. I wish you had let me fly out."

Anna forgave her father's exclusion of her when he agreed to take her on his next overseas trip. The navy had many rules; "no women on ships" was just one of them. As commander in chief, he would break the rules for his daughter on his next trip abroad.

Father and daughter were getting along so well that by the beginning of March 1944, Anna did not return to Seattle after the Christmas holidays but moved into the White House. She took over the Lincoln Suite on the second floor where Harry and Louise Hopkins had lived. Hopkins had taken the place of Roosevelt's political advisor when Louis Howe died in 1936. Both Hopkins and Missy knew the president's moods. Hopkins knew when his boss needed to push ahead with signing one more paper or seeing one more supplicant and when he needed to relax by playing cards or telling stories. Hopkins had lived at the White House for three and a half years, but near Christmas 1943 he and his wife moved out of the White House into their own home in Georgetown. With Harry gone and Missy ill, Roosevelt found the White House increasingly lonely. Eleanor was away most of the time visiting troops in training or when they returned home injured, or speaking to groups that the president couldn't. His sons were in the service. At cocktail time, FDR would ask an usher, "See who's home and ask them to stop in." When the reply came, "Sorry, Mr. President, there is no one home," the president of the United States ate by himself on a tray and then went to bed.

Franklin Roosevelt needed his daughter. She could provide the understanding smile or quick laugh to cheer him up. According to James, his mother was incapable of "that touch of triviality he needed to lighten his burden." Elliott observed, "Father could relax more easily with Anna than with Mother. He could enjoy his drink without feeling guilty. Though Mother had gotten to the point where she would think she was relaxing, she was always working."

Anna acted as his hostess at dinners, screened his visitors, and helped with his speeches. "I found myself trying to take over little chores that I felt would relieve Father of some of the pressure under which he was constantly working." Now that her husband worked at the Pentagon living at the White House seemed perfect. What would her mother think? "She personally would love it," as long as Anna realized that no one took over her position as first lady. Eleanor might travel a good deal, but she was still mistress of the White House, and no one was going to take that from her. She had often clashed with other women who had acted as hostess in her absence: James's first wife Betsey Cushing, Missy, and Louise Hopkins, Harry's wife. Even when Eleanor was around, Louise would plan the dinner parties down to the seating arrangements usurping Eleanor's position. Anna knew her mother, "This would annoy the pants off her."

Without title or salary, Anna did just about everything that the president asked of her. He would say, "Sis, you handle that," and she did. "It was immaterial to me whether my job was helping to plan the 1944 campaign, pouring tea for General de Gaulle or filling Father's empty cigarette case." Anna's son Johnny Boettiger called the father and daughter working relationship an "ideal match," "a perfect fit, hand in glove." Anna, at thirty-eight, was vibrant, bringing "young life in the White House" which according to Eleanor made "it a more cheerful place to anyone who happens to stay there." Anna did raise the spirits of those around her. Daisy Suckley described her, "She is a wonderful person; sympathetic, understanding, very intelligent, and full of fun."

Anna was well aware that the war was wearing her father down. He was often tired, but didn't sleep well. He suffered from headaches, he coughed excessively, and his hand shook when he tried to light a cigarette or sign a letter. His lip drooped. Anna cornered Ross McIntire, his personal physician. What was wrong with her father? McIntire tried to assure her that the president was recovering from flu and bronchitis. Anna didn't think the doctor, "really knew what he was talking about." McIntire was an ear, nose, and throat doctor who usually treated the president's chronic sinus problems.

For a week prior to March 25 the president was in and out of bed with a fever, yet he traveled to Hyde Park to meet Lucy. She was coming from New York on the following day. It had been merely a few days since her husband's death and funeral. According to Daisy Suckley's journal, ". . . he hopes to show her around the place, the Library, his cottage etc., so he took things easy—had a good nap before lunch, & after lunch sat in a deck chair in the sun." Not only lonely and in mourning, Lucy had myriad estate problems to settle, the types of things that Winty had always handled. Both FDR and Lucy needed the love and understanding of the other. Lucy spent the day with Franklin leaving around 6:30 in the evening. She worried about her ailing friend. She had just lost a husband; she feared losing Franklin after she had just found him again. After dinner, Roosevelt felt his temperature rising so he went to bed. He returned to Washington on March 28 for a medical examination.

Admiral Ross McIntire asked Lieutenant Commander Howard Bruenn, a cardiologist, to examine the president. Anna accompanied her sixty-two-year-old father that day to Bethesda Naval Hospital. "I suspected something was terribly wrong as soon as I looked at him," Bruenn stated. "His face was pallid and there was a bluish discoloration of his skin, lips and nail beds."

The results of Bruenn's examination were not good. Roosevelt's blood pressure was too high; his lungs held fluid; his heart was failing. Bruenn recalled, "There was then no specific drug to lower blood pressure, but they called for low doses of digitalis, a low-calorie diet, dining alone rather than with wearying guests, ten rather than twenty cigarettes a day, and only a drink and a half at cocktail time."

Other medical experts protested. "The president can't take time off to go to bed," McIntire insisted. Only when Bruenn threatened to resign did the president get the medication. McIntire, as the president's physician, chose to keep this information from the public in advance of the presidential election in 1944.

McIntire also forbade Bruenn to tell the president of his health, and surprisingly, Roosevelt never asked his doctors what was wrong, why he was taking medication. Neither did Eleanor want to admit his sickness. Her husband had overcome so much in the past; it didn't seem possible that he was deathly ill. "I don't think Mother saw it. She wasn't looking for him to be any different," Anna thought. Eleanor attributed her husband's poor health to "the weariness that assails everyone who grasps the full meaning of war as it is a physical ailment."

When Bernard Baruch heard that the president needed a place to rest away from the worries of the White House, he offered his 17,500-acre winter residence, Hobcaw Barony on the South Carolina coastline. Baruch, born in 1870, earned three dollars a week at his first job. By the time he was thirty, he was millionaire from his stock market investments. At one point, Roosevelt had offered to make him secretary of the treasury, but Baruch preferred to be an unofficial adviser and to continue to financially support the Democratic Party. Daisy said of Baruch, "He is . . . *notorious* for his succession of affairs with women. On the other hand, he is the soul of kindness and generosity, is constantly helping people. . . ."

Roosevelt accepted Baruch's invitation. Bruenn, McIntire, Edwin "Pa" Watson, Roosevelt's appointments secretary, and Admiral Leahy, his military representative, traveled with the president south to Hobcaw arriving April 9, Easter Sunday. Roosevelt's greatest wish? "I want to sleep and sleep, twelve hours a night." That he did. He went to bed early after dinner at seven and slept late in the morning. During the day Roosevelt rested, sailed, fished, and drove about the estate to observe the dogwoods, the crepe myrtle, deer, wild boar, and birds.*

---

*Baruch's daughter, Belle, inherited Hobcaw. At her death, it became part of a foundation created for the "purposes of teaching and/or research of forestry, marine biology, and the care and propagation of wildlife, flora, and fauna. . . ."

After Anna had moved the remainder of her things from Seattle to Washington, including her children, she joined her mother, Prime Minister, and Mrs. John Curtin of Australia and the president of Costa Rica, Teodor Picado. They flew to Hobcaw for lunch with Roosevelt. Eleanor remarked of his retreat at Hobcaw, "I came home feeling that it was the very best move Franklin could have made."

Whether she did or did not know that Lucy Rutherfurd was 140 miles away in Aiken, Eleanor returned to Washington. On April 28, Lucy traveled to Hobcaw, at Roosevelt's insistence, with her stepdaughter Alice and her stepson's wife. Now because Winty was no longer alive, she is listed in the official record as Lucy Rutherfurd and not Mrs. Paul Johnson. At lunch that day, Roosevelt sat at one end of the table, Baruch at the other. Lucy sat at Roosevelt's right. Baruch had even given up his war ration tickets for gasoline so Lucy could make the drive.

Only the news of the death of Secretary of the Navy Frank Knox marred the lunch. At seventy years old he had died of a heart attack. Despite his increasing strength, the president experienced abdominal pain and nausea after the luncheon possibly due to the sad news. It kept him in bed a few days. Bruenn ordered X-rays as soon as the group returned to Washington on May 7.

Eleanor cancelled her speaking engagements in New York to be at home with Franklin for the funeral, for she thought he would return to the White House. As she would be attending the funeral, Roosevelt stayed on at Hobcaw an extra week.

After D-Day, June 6, 1944, with Eleanor at Hyde Park for the summer, Roosevelt asked of Anna, "What would you think about our inviting an old friend of mine to a few dinners at the White House.* This would have to be arranged when your mother is

---

*Shoumatoff writes of a meeting between Lucy and FDR in the White House, sanctioned by Rutherfurd and Eleanor, when Roosevelt was very ill (p. 109). If this meeting took place, it would have to have been prior to Rutherfurd's illness in 1937.

away and I would have to depend on you to make the arrangements." He was speaking of Lucy, of course. Anna's first response was, "It was a terrible decision to have to make in a hurry." Anna knew the pain that her father's relationship with Lucy had caused her mother. Yet, for love of her father, she agreed. Lucy would visit over the weekend of July 7. She would come to the southwest gate across from the Executive Office Building. The guest list for the night Lucy visited would not be given to the press. Over the next nine months, FDR and Lucy would meet in the White House over a dozen times when Eleanor was away. On one such occasion, Franklin Jr., on leave from the navy, entered his father's office unannounced to find a strange woman massaging his father's legs. His father introduced her as "my old friend, Mrs. Winthrop Rutherfurd."

James described the renewed relationship of his father with the woman who was once "all he wanted."

> By this time he was in his sixties and she was in her fifties, and even if he had not been crippled, I doubt there would have been more than friendship between them. But it was a very real friendship and they shared the memory of a romance when both were young. He was a sentimental man and a good friend who was not about to forget Lucy even after life had drawn them apart. I am sure he needed a friend and felt she needed one. I suppose they could talk to one another as they could not talk to others.

Anna felt there was nothing "clandestine about these occasions. On the contrary, they were occasions which I welcomed for my father because they were light-hearted and gay, affording a few hours of much needed relaxation for a loved father and world leader in a time of crises. This period was from early 1944 to early 1945 when I accompanied Father to the Yalta Conference."

The two had originally intended to meet at Shangri-la, his mountain resort, but with General de Gaulle in Washington, FDR couldn't leave town. On the night of Friday, July 6, Lucy arrived at the White House at 8:45 and stayed until after eleven. Roosevelt left at 6:20 the next day and called for Lucy at her sister's home in Georgetown. Back at his White House study, they shared cocktails with Anna and her husband, John. Anna had not seen Lucy in twenty-eight years. She remembered little of her but that at ten or eleven years old, "I remember feeling happy and admiring when I was greeted one morning at home by Miss Lucy Mercer."

> Never did Father and I discuss or mention any "relationship" other than the one of friendship with which I was familiar. As for me, I still found Mrs. Rutherfurd to be a most attractive, stately, but warm and friendly person. She certainly had an innate dignity and poise which would command respect.

Alonzo Fields, the president's butler, sensed, "This was a special evening. You could feel that this was someone warm who cared a great deal about him." Johnny Boettiger, Anna's son said of his mother, grandfather, and Lucy, "The three of them had a capacity for loving humor, for having fun. It wasn't a tight, ironic sense of humor. It was a silly humor that didn't respect the boundaries they all imagined Eleanor would impose."

The next day Franklin and Lucy went to Shangri-la, the presidential retreat in Maryland seventy-five miles from Washington. Built by the Civilian Conservation Corps as a summer camp for boys and girls, it was fitted for the president's use in 1942. Because of the war, he could no longer cruise on the presidential yacht in open waters. He needed an alternative place to relax from Washington. The camp consisted of six oak cabins; the principal cabin for the president and his guests had a living and dining room, kitchen, four bedrooms, two bathrooms, and a screened-in porch. Roosevelt chose the name Shangri-la after the mythical, hidden land depicted in James Hilton's novel *Lost Horizon*. The compound would later become known as Camp David.

Sometimes Lucy and FDR met at a place where they had rendezvoused in the early days of their love, Oatlands near Leesburg, Virginia. Oatlands was the home of their mutual friend Edith Eustis. She would call Roosevelt to say, "There is someone here you want to see." Roosevelt would then make the drive from Washington into the Virginia countryside.

Lucy was forever grateful to Anna for allowing Franklin even a brief reprise from the burden of the war and for easing her loneliness after Rutherfurd's death. After Roosevelt died, Lucy wrote Anna, "[T]he strength of his beloved presence—so filled with loving understanding, so ready to guide and to help. I love to think of his very great pride in you. . . . I have been reading over some very old letters of his—and in one he says: 'Anna is a dear fine person—I wish so much that you knew her'—Well, now we do know one another—and it is a great joy to me & I think he was happy this past year that it was so. . . ."

As Lucy again dominated Roosevelt's emotional life, another woman who loved him was slipping away. Missy LeHand was with her sister at a movie theater in Harvard Square on Sunday evening, July 30. In those days a newsreel preceded the double feature. On the newsreel, Roosevelt was shown giving his acceptance speech from his railroad car in San Diego for his fourth nomination for president. Missy had not seen her former boss for several months. She was shocked at his weight loss, his haggard face with the dark circles under his eyes. Missy became agitated and they had to leave the theater. Back at her sister's home, she looked through old photographs of FDR when he was young and vigorous, and she wept. When her sister Ann looked in on Missy that night, she found her slumped over. Ann called an ambulance. Only forty-six years old, Missy died at Charles Naval Hospital from an embolism. Eleanor was in Hyde Park when she heard; FDR was sailing toward Alaska to visit troops. Missy's death affected him deeply. He suffered an attack of angina. "You and I lost a very dear friend," Tully declared. He replied, "Yes, poor Missy." He was close to tears, but as Tully knew, "He didn't want to show any emotion." In tribute to his old friend and helpmate, he had a cargo ship named in her honor. It was launched on March 27, 1945, just a few weeks before his own death. He sent the following message: "Mrs. Roosevelt and I send warm greetings to all who attend the launching of the *S.S. Marguerite A. LeHand* in the hope that a craft which bears so honored a name will make a safe journey and always find a peaceful harbor."

On August 23, 1944, FDR, Anna, Lucy, Barbara, and John Rutherfurd sat on the South Portico of the White House celebrating the liberation of Paris by having tea. The Labor Day weekend came the following week, and Roosevelt was kicking off his fourth run for the presidency. Friday, September 1, as the president was traveling from Washington to Hyde Park, he stopped off for several hours at Allamuchy, New Jersey to visit Lucy. He had his train, the *Ferdinand Magellan*, rerouted from the B & O line to the Pennsylvania-LeHigh line where the Hudson Railroad transected the Rutherfurd land.* When the three card-playing reporters on board were told the journey would be delayed a few hours, they didn't bother to check why the train was waylaid in New Jersey. His specially built elevator lowered the president from his private railroad car. He, his dog Fala, and Daisy Suckley got into his automobile with the Secret Service and drove toward the Rutherfurd estate. Lucy later told Elizabeth Shoumatoff that many people witnessed his visit, but it was not reported due to the wartime restrictions of keeping the president's location a secret. Roosevelt took advantage of that policy in his desire to see Lucy as often as he could.

*In *FDR's Last Year* (1974) Jim Bishop claims that Roosevelt also secretly rerouted his train to visit both Winty and Lucy in Aiken on his trips to Warm Springs.

The flurry of activity at the Rutherfurd home prior to Roosevelt's arrival belied the name "Tranquility." Bushes had to be trimmed, furniture dusted, a special bedroom was decorated complete with turned down linen sheets on the bed in case the president wanted to rest. Before Roosevelt arrived, an employee exclaimed, "You'd think the president was coming." "He is," Lucy simply stated. She even had a special phone installed to make and receive foreign calls. So close were Roosevelt and Lucy that even in time of war, he didn't mind her overhearing his calls with Churchill. He probably would not have extended this privilege to Eleanor who would have wanted to be part of the conversation. After Roosevelt's death, Lucy admitted to Charles E. Bonlen, Roosevelt's adviser on Russia and her friend, that the president had kept no wartime secrets or burdens from her.

Daisy Suckley noted in her diary for Friday, September 1, that the president's car was met by Lucy and her stepson John. "She is a *lovely* person, full of charm, and with beauty of character shining in her face; no wonder the Pres. has cherished her friendship all these years—" Daisy had first met Lucy in 1922 in Aiken when she proclaimed, "Mrs. R. is young & attractive, about 24, and seems to fit her place as a stepmother to the five children wonderfully." Daisy further remembered her as "tall & calm & pretty & *sad*, when her daughter was 6 mos. old, at Aiken.* She does not look sad now, but how little one knows about the inner life of others." She then notes, "The Pres. with all his intense interest in life & in people, with all his joking & teasing, sometimes, in repose, looks really sad."

Lucy was dressed in a black dress, black gloves, but without a hat or stockings. Daisy described Johnnie Rutherfurd as a "giant" and his wife "small & slender." Their twin boys, aged seven, found a string to tie up Fala and a bowl of water for him while

*Lucy was thirty-one when Barbara was born in 1922.

Roosevelt looked over the expansive acreage of Tranquility Farms giving advice on the property's trees. He always prided himself on his arbor knowledge, for he liked to call himself "just an old tree farmer."

The Secret Service wanted the president to be seated at the end of the luncheon table. Franklin wanted to be seated next to his Lucy. Guests at lunch included a former sister-in-law of Winthrop's who had remarried after her husband died; they lived at the older Rutherfurd house several miles away. Also at the table were Johnnie Rutherfurd and his wife, Georgette Rutherfurd, whose husband, Guy, was at the front, Alice Rutherfurd, and her husband, Arturo Ramos. Daisy's keen eye saw Ramos as "attractive & charming, but doesn't amount to a row of pins, as far as I can find out. . . ." Daisy described "a delicious lunch." "Mrs. Rutherfurd had planned for lobsters, but when the Pres. told her he had had lobsters the night before, & would have them again at Val-Kill this evening, she left them out." The presidential party left at 3:45. "It was a really a lovely day," recorded Daisy, "centering around Mrs. Rutherfurd, who becomes more lovely as one thinks about her—The whole thing was out of a book—a complete setting for a novel, with all the characters at that lunch table if one counts the absent husbands and wives etc."

FDR enjoyed the visit as much as Daisy had. He asked the Secret Service to investigate if the Allamuchy route could be used as an alternate way to Hyde Park. Agent Hassett described the visit in his journal and then crossed out the sections leaving only a businesslike narration of the detour. "Told the president the Secret Service satisfied with the Pennsylvania-Lehigh route. . . ." The only obstacle seemed to be that the train would pass over Hell's Gate Bridge in New York. "He said he would consider it; but he still wants another trip over Hell Gate—said he didn't believe the bridge would be blown up during his transit." Now he could visit Lucy more often on his way to Hyde Park.

After the president had left, Lucy walked about her yard and came across a man sitting on her lawn furniture. Agent Griffith had been guarding the rear entrance of the house. Lucy informed him that the president's party "had left about an hour ago." It took him the rest of the evening to catch up to the train.

Eleanor met the train at Hyde Park's Highland station at 6:45 that evening. On Labor Day, September 4, Roosevelt and Daisy drove to Top Cottage. They sat on the porch sometimes talking, "half the time, saying nothing." Roosevelt confided to Daisy that he felt "low" and "logy." "He didn't know what was the matter with him. . . ."

CHAPTER 14

"He seems very anxious to have his portrait done now"

On November 27, 1944, Roosevelt left for the Little White House in Warm Springs for the annual Thanksgiving dinner with his fellow polio patients. He planned to stay three weeks. This was his first long visit to Warm Springs since the United States had entered the war. Eleanor stayed in Washington. She hadn't wanted to go, and she felt she could stay behind as Laura Delano known as "Polly" and Margaret "Daisy" Suckley were going with Roosevelt.

Nicknamed "the handmaidens" by Eleanor, his two unmarried, distant cousins provided Franklin Roosevelt with much needed company in the last few years of his life. They made an interesting pair. Polly was the older, being born in 1890, but not by much, as Daisy was born in 1891. Polly was "a law unto herself," and "beautiful as a Dresden doll." She earned the name Polly because as a small child Apollinaire water was all she would drink. As an adult she died her hair blue, almost purple, and carefully painted a widow's peak on her forehead every morning. She jingled when she walked due to her many bracelets and large, chunky jewelry, "and rope upon rope of pearls." She loved red nail polish, rouge, and lipstick. She was flirty and had scandalized the family by once wanting to marry the son of a rich Japanese family. He was Otohiko Matsukata, the first secretary of the Japanese embassy. He had been FDR's Harvard classmate. When she didn't marry, she carried on with her chauffeur and bred and showed Irish setters and longhaired dachshunds.

In contrast, "Daisy was as homey as an old cardigan with her hair drawn back tight in a bun." She was gentle, intelligent, quiet but with a wicked sense of humor. She enjoyed her role in Roosevelt's life, her contrast to Polly, what she called, "my part of prim spinster." As a young woman, she had received several marriage proposals, but she didn't want to marry. As Polly, she loved FDR, and she also loved dogs.

She had given the president the Scottie, Fala, as a Christmas present in 1940. The dog, whose Secret Service name was Informer, accompanied the president everywhere and during the 1944 campaign became a point of controversy with the allegation that Roosevelt had left Fala in the Aleutian Islands and sent a destroyer to fetch him at a cost of millions. The president addressed the story at a Teamsters banquet. "These Republican leaders have not been content with attacks on me, or my wife, or on my sons. No, not content with that, they now include my little dog Fala." While his family didn't resent these attacks, Fala did, according to Roosevelt in a semiserious tone. When Fala supposedly heard the story of the destroyer sent to get him at taxpayers' expense, the president said, ". . . his Scotch soul was furious. He has not been the same dog since. I am accustomed to hearing malicious falsehoods about myself . . . but I think I have a right to resent, to object to libelous statements about my dog." Fala, who received applause when he descended the president's train, was a great crowd pleaser. Mike Reilly, who had guarded FDR since

1935, described the first dog as "the greatest little ham that ever walked on four feet."

Roosevelt enjoyed the company of both Daisy and Polly. "You're the only people I know that I don't have to entertain," was his tribute to them. Eleanor tolerated them as she had Missy because their companionship with her husband gave her freedom. Both Daisy and Polly knew of Franklin's renewed relationship with Lucy, and they approved. Elliott Roosevelt believed,

> Laura Delano had no patience with Mother or with anything she did. She believed that Mother had been the wrong choice as a wife for her cousin. Our tiny, bejeweled aunt felt sure that Lucy Mercer and Father should never have given up each other. She saw no reason why they should not begin to meet again.

Lucy and Barbara arrived at Warm Springs on Friday, December 1, minus Lucy's very old and large French maid. FDR had left special instructions with Hacky and Tully to make sure the maid was properly cared for at Warm Springs. Mother and daughter stayed in the guest cottage behind the main house. Daisy described Lucy, "perfectly lovely, tall, stately, & with the sweetest expression. She is much worried by the Pres. looks, finds him thin and tired looking." Daisy shared Lucy's concern for Franklin's health. Daisy thought Barbara "quite pretty," "tall and too thin," and "looking very serious for her age."

That evening the President mixed cocktails for all. It amused Daisy that Lucy ordered a weak old fashioned but that the president gave her another drink against her wishes. "She says she never took one until she was fifty, & can't get used to seeing Barbara taking them." Barbara was twenty-two years old and according to Daisy, "interested" in a young man recovering from a wound in Europe. The next morning the main house was cold and Lucy wore her furs over her pajama wrapper. FDR was in bed with his sweater on. Always concerned that he might catch a cold from a chill, Daisy got him an extra sweater and his coat.

On Saturday, December 2, Roosevelt took his guests for a ride. Lucy, Daisy, Polly, and Monty Anderson, another distant relative of FDR, went for a drive to Dowdell's Knob, which overlooked the Pine Mountain Valley. Barbara stayed behind in bed with a sore throat. Daisy was a bit perturbed that Lucy sat next to FDR in her usual spot and that "I am half hidden in the corner next to her—" Lucy later spoke of the afternoon to Anna. "I had the most fascinating hour I've ever had. He just sat there and told me of some of what he regarded as the real problems facing the world now. I just couldn't get over thinking of what I was listening to, and then he would stop and say, 'You see that knoll over there? That's where I did this-or-that,' or 'You see that bunch of trees?' Or whatever it was. He would interrupt himself, you, know. And we just sat there and looked."

The conversation was a revelation to Anna. She understood part of the attraction between Lucy and her father. "As Lucy said all this to me, I realized Mother was not capable of giving him this—just listening. And of course, this is why I was able to fill in for a year and a half, because I could listen."

Daisy found Lucy good for Franklin, "a *perfectly lovely person* in every way one can think of, and is a wonderful friend to him." As the two women got to know each other better, Daisy declared, "We understand each other perfectly, I think, and feel the same about F.D.R. She has worried & does worry, terribly, about him, & has felt for years that he has been terribly lonely. . . ." Both women commiserated over their concern over Franklin until, "We got to the point of literally weeping on each other's shoulder & we kissed each other, I think just because we each felt thankful that the other understood & wants to help Franklin!"

Lucy and Barbara went home on Sunday afternoon. Roosevelt drove them as far as Augusta with the Rutherfurd car following with Daisy. Daisy records that when they accidentally hit and killed a pig, the Secret Service agent paid the black family five dollars. The farmers were surprised because no one had ever paid them for running down their pigs or chickens. The Rutherfurds proceeded on their way. Roosevelt and his party returned to Warm Springs. As always, when Lucy left him, he felt "let down."

A week later Lucy wrote to Daisy. She realized the bond they shared in their love of Franklin Roosevelt, the man she called "the Source I Do Not Question." "[Y]ou can imagine how very wonderful it was for me to feel myself under the same roof and within the sound of the voice we all love after so many, many years." She asks her to visit her in Aiken when FDR goes to Yalta. "I lead a completely quiet life & you need no clothes—you could work on your beloved papers & perhaps I could help you!* Do say you will come."

The president left Warm Springs on Sunday, December 17, to head back to Washington. Lucy drove to Atlanta where she joined the presidential party returning to Washington.

On January 12, 1945, Lucy rode with FDR from Washington to Hyde Park. Daisy now refers to Lucy as "my new 'cousin.'" "She & I have one very big thing in common: our unselfish devotion to F."

On January 20, Roosevelt took the presidential oath of office for the fourth time. Because of the war, the order of the day was simplicity. When reporters asked why there would be no marching bands or drill teams, Roosevelt answered, "Who is there here to parade?" Mike Reilly of the Secret Service declared, "Dog catchers have taken office with more pomp and ceremony."

---

*Daisy worked tirelessly on organizing Roosevelt's presidential library at Hyde Park. The Franklin D. Roosevelt Library was the first of the presidential libraries. Previous presidential papers could be sold, destroyed, or remain with the family. The library was built on sixteen acres of Hyde Park land donated by FDR and his mother. Roosevelt opened up the museum portion of the building on June 30, 1941. Daisy identified photographs, letters, and documents for the library until her retirement in 1963. She died in 1991; she was one hundred years old.

James Roosevelt had come from the Philippines at his father's request and special orders to help him walk to the podium. James said to him, "Old man, you look like hell." His father laughed and replied, "I'm a little tired, that's all. A few days in Warm Springs will fix me right up."

The brief ceremonies took place on the South Portico of the White House. The snow of the previous evening had changed to sleet by the morning of the inauguration. Lucy observed this ceremony from the lawn of the White House along with eight thousand guests including some wounded servicemen. The wind was bitter but Roosevelt stood bareheaded in a plain blue business suit and delivered the shortest inaugural address of any president, just 573 words. He spoke of how the war had tested the American spirit. "If we meet that test—successfully and honorably—we shall perform a service of historic importance which men and women and children will honor throughout time."

After his speech was finished, Roosevelt confided to his son that he didn't think he could find the strength to greet two thousand people at the reception. Jimmy urged his father not to go, but Roosevelt insisted, "It would look bad to bow out. I don't dare shake the faith of the people. That's why I ran again, Jimmy. The people elected me their leader, and I can't quit in the middle of a war." He further told his son, "There's a bottle of bourbon up in my room. If you'll go up and sneak it down to me and I can get some inside of me, I think I can get through this."

Roosevelt also wanted to talk about his will with his son as he had named him one of the three executors, the only one from the family. He told James that there was a letter in his safe explaining his instructions for his funeral. James recalled:

> That conversation, of course, clearly indicates that he was thinking of death, but I took it to mean only that he was thinking of a death which had to come. Now that I look back, I realize why he insisted mother go to the trouble of having all thirteen

grandchildren at that inauguration, but I did not see that then. I did not suspect, when I left him, that I was embracing him for the last time.

Daisy recorded that although the president's right arm trembled, "It did us all good to see him standing there, straight & vigorous, thin but with good colour—All the sentimental ladies who love him were ready for tears! . . ." After the festivities, Daisy called on Lucy at her sister's home in Georgetown to give her the details of the reception because Lucy could not attend. Daisy returned to Marbury's the next day and Lucy accompanied her back to the White House.

Two days after his inauguration, Roosevelt left on a long journey to meet in secret with Churchill and Stalin at Yalta on the Black Sea. The three leaders would plan the end of the war and the postwar world. Although Eleanor had asked to accompany the president, he took Anna as he had promised her. He explained to his wife that because Churchill was bringing his daughter, it would be more seemly for Anna to accompany him. In reality Anna could do what Eleanor couldn't, provide a haven of understanding and support in the midst of tense negotiations. As the *U.S.S. Quincy* sailed past the Virginia coastline, Roosevelt and his daughter sat alone on the deck of the cruiser taking them as far as Malta. He talked of Virginia history and in the midst of describing birds that inhabited the shoreline he pointed, "over there is where Lucy grew up. That's where Lucy's family used to live. That's where they had their plantation."

Lucy stayed on his mind on the trip across the Atlantic. She and Daisy had put together a gift package for FDR's sixty-third birthday on January 30. On his seventh day at sea, he had forgotten his birthday until their package arrived on his breakfast tray. His present consisted of "a lot of little gadgets." There were napkins Daisy had purchased for his Warm Springs home, a pocket comb, a room thermometer, and a cigarette lighter that worked in the wind. The thought the two women put into making his birthday special was the best gift.

The conference took place at Lividia Palace once the summer home of Czar Nicholas II. While Roosevelt settled into the czar's bedroom, Lucy wrote Daisy from her home in Aiken where she had moved into a smaller house. With Winty's death and her family grown and gone, Ridgeley Hall was too large and too empty. The Pinkerton family, descendants of the founder of the detective agency, had built Lucy's new home, named Tip Top Too, in the late 1920s. Daisy is the writer, Lucy laments, "One of the world's best correspondents seems now in communication with one of the world's worst—" "I feel as though I could scrub this little house from garret to cellar (if it had any) and do any physical thing—but my desk frightens me—" She congratulates Daisy on Fala's impending fatherhood, for Daisy's dog, Button, was about to have puppies. Lucy asks Daisy to keep her informed. "Write soon—and tell me whatever news you have as you are in official touch & I am not."

The news from Yalta was that Roosevelt's health was not good. The photographs of the three leaders show Roosevelt thin, his face drawn, dark circles under his eyes. Daisy records in her diary, "I am really worried about F.D.R. Even the papers say 'his aides are worried about his health.' In all the pictures that have come out, he looks really sick. . . ." Lord Moran, Churchill's doctor, wrote "To a doctor's eye, the President appears a very sick man. He has all the symptoms of hardening of the arteries of the brain in an advanced stage, so that I give him only a few months to live."

Roosevelt returned home on February 26 and addressed a joint session of Congress on March 1, 1945, to report on Yalta. For the first time the president was rolled down the aisle in his wheelchair, and he gave his address seated in a chair on the floor in front of the dais. He asked Congress to "pardon" his addressing them while seated, "but I know that you will realize that it makes it a lot easier for me in not having to carry about ten pounds of steel around on the bottom of my legs; and also because I have just completed a fourteen thousand mile trip." In his fourth term as president, the old rule of never allowing the true extent of his disability to show was starting to take too much energy to conceal.

In mid-March Lucy traveled once again to Washington to see Roosevelt. Her life now revolved around the times when Eleanor was away, so she could see Franklin. As in the past she stayed with her sister Violetta and her brother-in-law William Marbury. Eleanor was in North Carolina at an education conference. Monday afternoon, on March 12, he picked her up at her sister's home. They went for a ride through the Virginia countryside and later had dinner with Anna and her husband John in the president's study. Lucy ate dinner the following evening with Anna, John, and McKenzie King, the Canadian prime minister. Lucy lunched with Roosevelt and Anna the next day, and she returned for a three-hour meal alone with him that evening. Eleanor returned on Thursday.

At home again, Lucy asked Elizabeth Shoumatoff, who was in Aiken painting various commissions, to do a portrait of one of her step-grandsons. "There was somebody who asked very much about you. He seems very anxious to have his portrait done now." Shoumatoff who had seen the photos from Yalta declared Roosevelt to look "ghastly." Lucy responded as a woman in love, "Having lost so much weight, his features, always handsome, are more definitely chiseled."

On March 31 Lucy wrote Daisy to congratulate her on the arrival of Fala's offspring. Franklin and Eleanor had journeyed to Hyde Park to see the puppies the previous week. Lucy wrote, "I am glad that the trip [to Yalta] is over & that happy, peaceful days lie ahead—Please God they will be beneficial in a big way & that nothing—not even Germany's collapse—will interrupt."

Early in April after Easter, Lucy called Shoumatoff to inform her that the president would sit for his portrait while he rested at Warm Springs. To save on rationed gasoline, Shoumatoff would drive to Aiken with her photographer Robbins to pick up Lucy. Then all would travel on to Warm Springs.

Robbins and Shoumatoff arrived at Aiken late on Sunday evening, April 8. Lucy told them of the next day's plans. "We will leave directly after luncheon. The president telephoned that he will meet us in Macon at four o'clock. So we will be in Warm Springs for dinner."

Due to poor directions on Robbins's part, or so Shoumatoff believed, they "reached Macon way after four o'clock" on April 9. They could not locate the president's party. Nervously, Lucy powdered her nose and declared, "Nobody loves us, nobody cares for us." They could do nothing but drive toward their destination. As they entered Greenville just outside of Warm Springs, they saw the president of the United States in his open car drinking Coca-Cola in front of a corner drugstore with a crowd around him. Shoumatoff recorded, "The expression of joy on FDR's face upon seeing Lucy made all the more striking the change I saw in him since I painted him in 1943. My first thought was: how could I make a portrait of such a sick man?"

CHAPTER 15

"One of the greatest men that ever lived"

In a little over a year, Lucy had lost Winty, her husband, and Franklin, the man she'd wanted as her husband. The nation had lost a president. Eleanor had lost a husband and her political partner; indeed, she had to face the loss of trust in her own family as well.

The sixty-three-year-old president died around 3:30 P.M. William Hassett, Roosevelt's assistant, called the White House to tell Press Secretary Steve Early. They must inform Eleanor. Dr. McIntire had called her earlier to say the president had fainted. McIntire suggested she keep her four o'clock speaking engagement and then leave for Warm Springs that evening. Upon finishing her speech, she was called to the telephone. Steve Early "asked me to come home at once. I did not even ask why. I knew down in the heart that something dreadful had happened. Nevertheless the amenities had to be observed, so I went back to the party. . . ." When the celebrated pianist Evelyn Tyner finished her piece, Eleanor rose to announce that she had to return to the White House. "In my heart I knew what had happened, but one does not actually formulate these terrible thoughts until they are spoken. I went to my sitting room and Steve Early and Dr. McIntire came to tell me the news."

Anna, at the hospital with her ill son, had also heard from Dr. McIntire that her father had fainted. When she returned to the White House, she found her mother in her sitting room already dressed in black. Eleanor cabled her four sons all still in service and sent for Vice-President Harry Truman.

Truman arrived at the White House at 5:30 P.M. and was taken to the first lady's sitting room. With her were Steve Early, Anna, and her husband John Boettiger. Eleanor put her arm around Truman's shoulder and said, "Harry, the President is dead." Too shocked to speak at first, Truman finally asked, "Is there anything I can do for you?" Eleanor replied, "Is there anything *we* can do for *you*? For you are the one in trouble now."

After only eighty-three days as vice-president, Truman had become the thirty-third president of the United States. He later described his emotions, "I felt like the moon, the stars, and all the planets had fallen on me." Eleanor witnessed the swearing in ceremony held in the Cabinet Room with the assembled Cabinet members before she left to fly to Warm Springs. She arrived at midnight as the rest of the country was coming to grips with the president's death. He'd been president for twelve years through the Depression, the New Deal, and into World War II. For both friends and enemies, it was as if he had always been president. Michael Reilly may have voiced it best, "I never really thought he'd die, until he did."

At the Little White House Eleanor calmly asked Daisy, Polly, and Tully what had happened. Daisy described crocheting when the president was stricken, Tully said that she was getting ready for lunch, but Polly told the truth. According to Eleanor's niece Eleanor Wotkyns, "It was a malicious thing to do, but very fitting of her." "She was a small, petty woman, jealous all her life of Eleanor's great success." Polly's reasoning was classic for her, "Eleanor would have found out anyway."

Eleanor spent five minutes in the bedroom, door closed, where her husband lay. On her return Tully noted, "Her eyes were dry again, her face grave but composed." She then questioned Polly on how often Franklin had seen Lucy and who had known of these meetings. Polly did not spare the details. It was obvious that Franklin had not kept his promise to Eleanor to foreswear Lucy. Then the coup de grace came, Anna had not only known about, but had arranged some of the meetings. Anna knew how much Franklin and Lucy's love had wounded her mother, and still she betrayed her. Eleanor must have felt that she had found those love letters all over again.

Upon returning to Washington with Roosevelt's body, Eleanor confronted her daughter, for now she could not confront her husband as she had done years ago. "Mother was so upset about everything and now so upset with me." Anna feared her mother would never forgive her. She tried to assure her mother that her father had asked her to invite Mrs. Rutherfurd to the White House. With all the pressures on him, she only wanted to help. "It was all above board. There were always people around," she said to justify her actions.

James empathized with Anna's awkward position. He later wrote, "I doubt that father felt he was doing anything wrong in seeing Lucy, but I certainly can understand his keeping it a secret because he believed mother would take it badly and would be hurt. She *was* hurt when she found out about it." He realized, "Mother was angry with Anna. . . . But what was Anna to do? Should she have refused Father what he wanted?"

> A child caught between two parents can only pursue as honorable a course as possible. Anna could no more serve as mother's spy on father than she could as father's spy on

mother. Anna suffered some private anguish, but she was as true as she could be to both our parents and she was blameless in this matter. Mother spent very little time with him during those last years. Anna did. So, too, at times, did Daisy and Polly. Lucy was there, too. And until her fatal illness, Missy.

Going through Franklin's effects at Hyde Park, Eleanor found the small watercolor of FDR painted by Shoumatoff at the White House. She had Daisy send it to Lucy. Lucy responded to Eleanor early in May.

> Thank you so very much. You must know that it will be treasured always. I have wanted to write you for a long time to tell you that I had seen Franklin and of his great kindness about my husband when he was desperately ill in Washington, & of how helpful he was too, to his boys—and that I hope very much that I might see you again—I can't tell you how deeply I feel for you and how constantly I think of your sorrow—you—whom I have felt to be the most blessed and privileged of women must now feel immeasurable grief and pain and they must be almost unbearable. . . .

Eleanor had made the kind overture, but that was all. If she replied to Lucy or contacted her further in any way, it's not known for certain.* She had been Franklin's wife, not Lucy.

Later that same week, Anna telephoned Lucy for the first time since her father's death. Lucy had been grieving, too. "I did not know that it was in me just now to be so glad to hear the sound of any voice—and to hear you laugh—was beyond words wonderful." Lucy's letter helped Anna cope with the loss of her father and her estrangement with her mother.

> "I had not written before for many reasons—but you were constantly in my thoughts & with very loving and heart torn

*Jon Meacham in his *Franklin and Winston* (2003) notes that the abbreviation "ans," is in the corner of Lucy's letter to Eleanor (p. 358).

> sympathy & I was following every step of the way. This blow must be crushing to you—to all of you—but I know that you meant more to your Father than any one and that makes it closer & harder to bear. It must be an endless comfort to you that you were able to be with him so much this past year."

For Anna the letter confirmed that her father loved her and if returning his love meant arranging for him to see Lucy, so be it.

> "He told me so often & with such feeling of all that you had meant of joy & comfort on the trip to Yalta. He said you had been so extraordinary & what a difference it made to have you. He told me of your charm & your tact—& of how everyone loved you. He told how capable you were & how you forgot nothing & of the little typewritten chits he would find at this place at the beginning or end of the day—reminding him of all the little or big things that he was to do. I hope he told you these things—but sometimes one doesn't. In any case you must have known—words were not needed between you."

Then Lucy let Anna know what Franklin had meant to her.

> "The world has lost one of the greatest men that ever lived—to me—the greatest. He towers above them all—effortlessly—& even those who openly opposed him seem shocked into the admission of his greatness. Now he is at peace—but he knew even before the end—that the task was well done."

Anna kept the letter in her bedside table the rest of her life only taking it out occasionally to show a few people.

Lucy remained close to Daisy in the days following Roosevelt's death. They shared the bond of two women who loved the same man outside the confines of his immediate family. When Daisy sent her photographs of Top Cottage, Lucy replied, "I have looked at them long . . . and they are good." More photographs sent by Daisy, this time from FDR's and Lucy's last days together, prompted, "I love having the one from Warm Springs—though they make the pain in one's heart even sharper."

Daisy even enlisted Lucy's help in organizing FDR's papers at Hyde Park. Did Lucy know the location of a diary kept by Franklin on his trip to Europe in 1918? The request must have stirred bittersweet memories of a time before Eleanor's discovery of their love letters. Lucy did not know where the diary was, but felt it would be in either Franklin's or Eleanor's papers. She refers Daisy to "Eddie MacCauley" who would know where the diary was as he was on the trip. She did recall particulars of FDR's trip to World War I Europe as assistant secretary of the navy for the dates of July 9–27, 1918. She informs Daisy that the diary describes his trip to Europe on the *Dyer*. She breaks down the trip to describe what FDR was doing on certain days that included a stay in London where he called on George V and met Churchill and even "spoke—I think—at a Gray's Inn dinner?" She was obviously well aware of the diary's existence and what it contained, "Let me know if you do not find it," she hastily ends the letter, "I must run as they are calling me. With love, Lucy."

On June 9, 1945, Anna arranged for Lucy to visit Roosevelt's grave at Hyde Park. The grave was not yet open to the public. Lucy drove from Allamuchy with her friend, Mrs. Kittredge. Not until Daisy informed her later did Lucy know that her visit had caused a stir among security. Anna had provided a card of admission for Lucy to visit the gravesite. When the lieutenant in charge of the guard received the card, he was perturbed that neither Mrs. Roosevelt nor Mr. Palmer, the new superintendent, had signed the card. By that time, Lucy and her friend had already departed or as Daisy noted in her daybook, "The ladies had got safely away however!"

Lucy wrote Daisy on June 19 from Allamuchy, "It distresses me that you were given so much trouble by my descent upon you. I had been lead to believe that I could slide in and out again without being a burden to anyone—" Visiting Franklin's grave affected Lucy, "The memory will be with me always." Daisy had invited

Lucy to her home at Wilderstein just twelve miles from Hyde Park, but the pain of returning to the Roosevelt's beloved Hudson Valley was too fresh. Lucy replied, "You know how much I should like to—and someday perhaps I may be able to ask you if you will have me—but you—who know all of the facts—will understand that just now I do not feel I should go." Lucy does reverse the invitation and asks Daisy to visit her as soon as possible. She's even willing to pick Daisy up and return her home. "Will you let me know what your best time would be and I shall make my time to suit you." She ends the letter, "With my love—Dear Margaret—and again my thanks—for the letter—and for your help."

Lucy resumed her quiet life rotating between Aiken and Allamuchy. Only Elizabeth Shoumatoff sought to remind her of that fatal afternoon by consulting her on details for the Roosevelt's portrait when he had been struck by the fatal cerebral hemorrhage. Lucy remembered that he had been wearing a blue tie.

Roosevelt was not easy to forget. After his death, Lucy sought validation of her relationship with him just as Anna had desired. Betsey Cushing, who had once been married to James Roosevelt, was now married to John Hay Whitney. They often stayed with friends in Aiken. Lucy would invite her to tea because of their shared life with FDR. Betsey Whitney said that Lucy had confided in her. She had loved Winty, was grateful to him, but Roosevelt had been the love of her life. Furthermore, according to Betsey, Lucy wanted to know if FDR had ever loved another woman physically as he had loved her. When the lights in the house went out, Betsey was relieved. "It must have been Franklin, she thought, annoyed at the line of questioning."

Lucy enjoyed her role as grandmother to her stepchildren's offspring. One year less a day, after she had gone to Warm Springs, her own daughter Barbara married Robert Knowles, Jr. on April 8,

1946, in a Catholic ceremony at the home of the George Meads, The Pillars.*

She still visited her cousins the Hendersons in North Carolina. Lyman Cotten, Jr., the boy who had so enjoyed her wedding cake, was now a professor of English at the University of North Carolina, where Lucy's niece, Lucy Mercer Marbury named for her, had graduated in 1944.

In November 1947, her sister Violetta came to Aiken in distress. William wanted a divorce to marry Marguerita Pennington who had been one of Lucy's and Violetta's classmates in Austria so many years ago. Violetta shot herself in the head on November 11 and Marbury was free to remarry. She was fifty-six years old.

On Christmas Day, Lucy's mother died in the Rockville sanitarium. For a woman who had stopped having birthdays when she was twenty-five, she'd had nearly sixty years beyond her declaration. She was buried at Arlington National Cemetery with her husband and her grandson.

Minna who had battled the Veterans Administration over her pension check for years left that task to Lucy. Lucy got a check for her mother for sixty dollars. She wrote, "Will you let me know if there is anything further to be done about this? Her last check was received by me and not cashed—but at the moment I have mislaid it—I think it was dated Dec. 31st, 1947, but I do not remember. Will communicate with you when I find it." Lucy didn't find it, and by March 1948 Minna was still receiving checks, and Lucy still returning them.

Early in 1948 Lucy began to tire easily, had lost her appetite, and was frequently ill. Considering all that she had lived through in the past few years, it was easy to say her symptoms were due to depression. By the time leukemia was diagnosed, the disease

*According to Shoumatoff, the Meads were the only ones in Aiken who knew that Lucy had been with Roosevelt the day he died.

was progressing rapidly. She entered Memorial Hospital in New York City. Physicians could do little for her except to lessen her pain with morphine. She died on Saturday, July 31, 1948, at the age of fifty-seven.

"Grace Tully wired me when Lucy Rutherford [*sic*] died. . . . She was a wonderful person and it makes me sad that I will not be able to see her again," Anna wrote to Daisy.

In Lucy's obituary, the *New York Times* devoted more space to her husband and his first wife than they did to her life. Lucy wouldn't have minded, she had always put others before herself.

One summer afternoon many years earlier, Lucy had been riding around the countryside near Tranquility. When she and her daughter, her sister, her brother-in-law, and her niece, came across a woman selling flowers and vegetables by the side of the road, Lucy demanded the automobile stop. She then bought all the woman had. To those in the car it seemed ridiculous as Lucy had all the vegetables and flowers in the world grown by herself and gardeners at her own home. Why had she stopped? Her reasoning was simple; the woman eking out a living by the side of the road could now go home.

Lucy could now go home. She was buried next to her husband. Of Roosevelt who had been her lover and later her friend, she had said at his death, "Now he is at peace." In the countryside of Tranquility, Lucy was now at peace.

NOTES

ABBREVIATIONS USED IN THE NOTES

JD	Jonathan Daniels
ARH	Anna Roosevelt Halsted
ER	Eleanor Roosevelt
FDR	Franklin Delano Roosevelt
SDR	Sara Delano Roosevelt

DOCUMENTS CITED FROM THE FRANKLIN DELANO ROOSEVELT LIBRARY (FDRL IN THE NOTES)

Anna Roosevelt Halsted Papers
Lorena Hickok Papers
Joseph P. Lash Papers
Lucy Mercer Naval Record
Minnie Mercer Pension File
Roosevelt Family: Papers Donated by the Children
Lucy Mercer Rutherfurd File
Rutherfurd Family File
White House Usher's Diary

INTRODUCTION

PAGE

xiv "such a great romantic story . . .": Jonathan Daniels to Anna Roosevelt Halstead, Nov. 19, 1963, Box 13, Folder 4, Halsted Papers, FDRL.

xiv "I feel that those . . .": ARH to JD, Nov. 14, 1963, Box 13, Folder 4, Halsted Papers, FDRL.

xiv "the story should be . . ." ibid.

xiv "I know you must write . . .": ARH to JD, July 4, 1966, Box 13, Folder 4, Halsted Papers, FDRL.

xv "One cannot help wonder . . .": unpublished article, Box 84, Folder 1, Halsted Papers, FDRL.

xv "were good friends . . .": "Thinks That FDR Wanted to Marry Lucy the Lovely", *Daily News*, August 13, 1966.

xv "Yet, if father loved . . .": James Roosevelt, *My Parents* (1976), p. 103.

xv "Never was there anything . . .": unpublished article, Box 84, Folder 1, Halsted Papers, FDRL.

xv "My mother . . . and my father . . .": ibid., *Daily News*, August 13, 1966.

xv "He might have been . . .": Eleanor Roosevelt, *This I Remember* (1949), p. 149.

CHAPTER 1

PAGE

1 "Inexorably drawn . . .": Elizabeth Shoumatoff, *FDR's Unfinished Portrait* (1990), p. 109.

1 "not give him . . .": Geoffrey C. Ward, *A First-Class Temperament: The Emergence of Franklin Roosevelt* (1989), p. 413.

2 "smiling face . . .": Bernard Asbell, *When F.D.R. Died* (1961), p. 36.

2 April 12, 1945 dawned . . . : Theo Lippman, Jr. *The Squire of Warm Springs* (1977), pp. 28–29.

2 Roosevelt returned by train . . . : Doris Kearns Goodwin, *No Ordinary Time* (1994), p. 598.

2 At the top of the list . . . : ibid.

3 "I was grateful . . .": Anna Boettiger letter, Box 84, Halsted Papers, FDRL.

3 "worst looking man . . .": Asbell, *When F.D.R. Died*, p. 14.
3 "dead weight . . .": Michael F. Reilly, *Reilly of the White House* (1947), pp. 226–27.
3 "There is something . . .": Shoumatoff, p. 98.
3 "He has such a remarkable . . .": ibid, p. 80.
4 It was in Georgia that FDR . . . : Lippman, pp. 87–88.
5 "Lucy is so sweet . . .": Geoffrey C. Ward, Ed. *Closest Companion: The Unknown Story of the Intimate Friendship between Franklin Roosevelt and Margaret Suckley* (1995), p. 416.
5 "Lucy was a wonderful . . .": Bernard Asbell, *Mother and Daughter: The Letters of Eleanor and Anna Roosevelt* (1988), p. 87.
5 "Mona Lisa smile . . .": Asbell, *When F.D.R. Died*, p. 32.
5 "There was a hint of fire . . . .": Elliott Roosevelt and James Brough, *An Untold Story: The Roosevelts of Hyde Park* (1973), p. 82.
5 "lovely"; "immature—like a character . . .": Ward, Ed. *Closest Companion*, pp. 415–16.
6 "in the presence of FDR . . .": Shoumatoff, pp. 102–3.
6 "He really should have . . .": ibid., p. 108.
6 Shoumatoff was in the habit . . . : ibid., p. 114.
6 "the United Nations Charter! . . .": ibid., p. 106.
7 "Oh, no, I'll be through . . .": ibid., p. 115.
7 "That gray look. . .": ibid., p. 116.
7 "The last thing I remember. . .": Asbell, *When F.D.R. Died*, p. 36.
7 "fifteen more minutes. . .": Shoumatoff, pp. 117–18.
8 Margaret Suckley's account: Geoffrey C. Ward, Ed. *Closest Companion*, pp. 416–19.
8 "We must pack . . .": Shoumatoff, p. 119.
9 "The expression . . .": ibid., p. 120.
9 Shoumatoff feared the notoriety . . . : ibid., p.126.
10 "I have burned . . .": ibid., pp. 72–73.

CHAPTER 2

PAGE

11 Their ancestors had lived . . . : Geoffrey C. Ward, *A First Class Temperament: The Emergence of Franklin Roosevelt* (1989), p. 359.
11 At about the same time . . . : Frank Freidel, *Franklin D. Roosevelt: A Rendezvous with Destiny* (1990), p. 4.

11 She liked to tell anyone . . . : Blanche Wiesen Cook, *Eleanor Roosevelt, Vol. I: 1884–1933* (1992), pp. 143–44.

11 On the western side . . . : Franklin D. Mares, *Springwood* (1993), p. 7.

12 The Mercers gave their name . . . : Joseph Alsop, *FDR, A Centenary Remembrance* (1982), p. 68.

12 The Hudson River Valley . . . : Freidel, pp. 4–5.

12 James Roosevelt, Franklin's father . . . : Mares, p. 6.

12 Lucy's grandfather . . . : Jonathan Daniels, *Washington Quadrille*, (1968), p. 23.

13 By the time . . . : Ward, p. 359.

13 "so rich and beautiful . . .": Daniels, p. 24.

13 Information on Minnie Tunis and Carroll Mercer from Minnie Mercer Pension File, FDRL.

13 "the most beautiful woman . . .": Ward, p. 359.

13 "This is my birthday, . . .": Daniels, p. 26.

13 "She certainly does look . . .": ibid.

14 Mercer's ship . . . : Daniels, pp. 27–28.

14 "cave dwellers, . . .": Elliott Roosevelt and James Brough, *An Untold Story: The Roosevelts of Hyde Park* (1973), p. 74.

14 She loved her reputation . . . : Ward, p. 360.

15 "to be invited . . .": Daniels, p. 33.

15 While his wife . . . : Ward, p. 360.

15 It was into this atmosphere . . .": Daniels, p. 29.

15 "Pooh, they just . . .": Daniels, p. 34.

15 "rich in heritage . . .": confidential source.

16 Here Lucy's parents . . . : Ward, p. 360.

16 Information on Lucy's schooling in Austria is from a confidential source.

16 Minnie and Carroll . . . : Daniels, p. 68.

CHAPTER 3

PAGE

19 "that it took me such endless . . .": Eleanor Roosevelt, *This Is My Story* (1937), p. 209.

19 "the same Washington parties . . .": James Roosevelt with Bill Libby, *My Parents: A Differing View* (1976), p. 100.

19 "which she knew . . .": Elliott Roosevelt and James Brough, *An Untold Story: The Roosevelts of Hyde Park* (1973), p. 22.

20 "a lady . . .": ibid., p. 73.

20 "of dark velvet . . ." : Bernard Asbell, *Mother and Daughter: The Letters of Eleanor and Anna Roosevelt* (1988), p. 24.

20 "I think she was . . .": Wesley Pruden, Jr., "Home-Town View On Lucy-FDR: It Can't Be True," *The National Observer*, August 1966.

20 "Ah, the lovely . . .": Nathan Miller, *FDR: An Intimate History* (1983), p. 113.

20 "She and Mother . . .": Roosevelt and Brough, p. 73.

20 "I remember feeling . . .": John R. Boettiger, Jr., *A Love in Shadow* (1978), p. 256.

20 Elliot described his grandmother . . . : Roosevelt and Brough, p. 73.

21 "Arrived safely . . .": Franklin D. Roosevelt, *FDR: His Personal Letters.* Vol.1, *The Early Years*, Ed., Elliott Roosevelt (1947), p. 219.

21 Roosevelt described her . . . : ibid., p. 220.

21 "inexorably drawn . . . :" Elizabeth Shoumatoff, *FDR's Unfinished Portrait* (1990), p. 109.

21 The face Lucy . . . : ibid., p. 80.

21 "She had the same . . .": Roosevelt and Brough, p. 73.

21 "You couldn't find two . . .": Anna Halsted interview, Lash Papers, FDRL.

22 Information on Eleanor Roosevelt's childhood from *This Is My Story* (1937), pp. 1–5.

22 "Mother had performed . . .": Roosevelt and Brough, p. 81.

22 "an ordeal . . .": Bernard Asbell, *The FDR Memoirs* (1973), p. 247.

23 "Eleanor and Franklin . . .": Geoffrey C. Ward, *A First Class Temperament: The Emergence of Franklin Roosevelt*, (1989), p. 415.

23 "Of course he was . . .": ibid., *The National Observer*, August 1966.

23 "She and Franklin . . .": Jonathan Daniels, *Washington Quadrille* (1968), p. 145.

CHAPTER 4

PAGE

24 "I just loved it, . . .": Blanche Wiesen Cook, *Eleanor Roosevelt, Vol. I: 1884–1933* (1992), p. 224.

24 As part of the Comforts Committee . . . : Jonathan Daniels, *Washington Quadrille* (1968), p. 114.

NOTES FOR PAGES 25–30

25 "She tells me . . .": ER to FDR, Family Papers, July 1916, Box 15, FDRL.
25 Twenty years later . . . : Elliott Roosevelt and James Brough, *An Untold Story: The Roosevelts of Hyde Park* (1973), p. 83.
25 Elliott Roosevelt recalled . . . : ibid., p. 84.
26 Another often-repeated story. . . : Joseph Alsop, *FDR: A Centenary Remembrance*, (1982), p. 67.
26 "Isn't it horrid. . .": Roosevelt and Brough, ibid., p. 83.
26 "a man I loved. . .": Geoffrey C. Ward, *A First Class Temperament: The Emergence of Franklin Roosevelt*, (1968), pp. 362–63.
26 A week after the excursion. . . : Lucy Mercer Naval Record, FDRL.
27 "goosy girl. . .": FDR to ER, July 16, 1917, Elliott Roosevelt, ed. *FDR: His Personal Letters*, Vol. II, (1947), p. 347.
27 "How to Save in Big Homes," *New York Times*, July 17, 1917.
27 "All I can say is . . .": *Letters*, vol. 2, pp. 349–50.
27 "I feel dreadfully. . .": ER to FDR, July 24, 1917, FDRL.
28 "a funny party. . .": Daniels, p. 119.
28 "I don't think you read. . .": ER to FDR, July 24, 1917, FDRL.
28 "Remember I *count* . . .": Roosevelt and Brough, ibid., 89.
28 "part of the family": Kenneth S. Davis, *FDR: The Beckoning of Destiny, 1882–1928* (1971), p. 488.
28 Eleanor sent Lucy . . . : Roosevelt and Brough, ibid., p. 89.
28 "I've written Miss Mercer . . .": Ted Morgan, *FDR: A Biography* (1985), p. 205.
29 "*You* are entirely . . .": *Letters*, Vol.II, p. 361.
29 "Lucy Mercer went . . .": Jonathan Daniels, *The End of Innocence* (1954), p. 237.
29 "the love of her life . . .": Alsop, p. 68.
29 "I can either run . . ."; "If you can't say . . .": Michael Teague, *Mrs. L: Conversations with Alice Roosevelt Longworth* (1981), p. ix.
30 "I want you to know . . .": ibid., p. 128.
30 "She always wanted . . .": ibid., p. 155.
30 "He'd rather be tight . . .": Betty Boyd Caroli, *The Roosevelt Women* (1998), p. 407.
30 "Aurora Borah Alice . . .": Cook, p. 221.
30 "beautiful, charming . . .": Teague, p. 157.
30 "He *deserved* . . ." Ward, p. 366.

30 "I saw you . . .": Joseph P. Lash, *Eleanor and Franklin* (1971), pp. 225–26.
31 "often, I used to think, . . .": Alsop, p. 69.

CHAPTER 5

PAGE

32 Information on Carroll Mercer's death from Jonathan Daniels, *Washington Quadrille* (1968), p. 124, 155–56, and Minnie Mercer Pension File, FDRL.
33 "I don't think . . .": Michael Teague, *Mrs. L: Conversations with Alice Roosevelt Longworth* (1981), p. 158.
34 On October 5, 1917. . .": Daniels, p. 125.
34 "The gossip . . .": ibid., p. 130.
34 Washington whispered . . . : ibid., p. 132.
34 "Don't telegraph, . . .": Elliott Roosevelt and James Brough, *An Untold Story: The Roosevelts of Hyde Park* (1973), p. 85.
35 "This afternoon I went . . .": ER to FDR, n.d. 1918, Box 15, FDRL.
35 "that it will . . .": Roosevelt and Brough, p. 91.
35 "People of social position . . .": ibid., p. 86.
35 "I thought: after all . . .": SDR to FDR and ER, Oct., 14, 1917, Elliott Roosevelt, Ed. *FDR: His Personal Letters, Vol. 2* (1947), pp. 274–75.
36 "I may continue . . .": ibid.
36 "I shall never . . .": Teague, p. 158.
36 "Very few mothers . . .": ER to SDR, January 22, 1918, FDRL.
36 "fine, and her smile. . .": Daniels, p. 157.
37 "She was with me . . .": ibid.
37 When he planned to volunteer . . . : Roosevelt and Brough, pp. 92–93.
37 "Sometimes I wondered . . .": ibid., p. 91.
37 "a temptation . . .": ER to FDR, July 1918, Box 15, FDRL.
38 "My husband did not . . .": Eleanor Roosevelt, *This Is My Story* (1937), p. 268.
38 "The bottom dropped . . .": Joseph P. Lash, *Eleanor and Franklin* (1971), p. 220.
39 "Eleanor was not willing . . .": Daniels, pp. 145–47.
39 It was a real love. . .": ibid.
39 "preferred a divorce . . .": Roosevelt and Brough, p. 95.

39 "well-kept secret. . .": ibid., 101.
39 Conjecture on the motel receipt from a confidential source.
40 Anna wrote . . . : Anna Roosevelt Halsted Papers, Box 84, Folder 1, FDRL.
40 "Always remember . . .": Teague, p. 158.
40 footnote "after considering . . .": Geoffrey C. Ward, *A First Class Temperament: The Emergence of Franklin Roosevelt* (1968), p. 413.
41 "It was all very well for you, . . .": ibid.
41 If FDR had divorced . . . : Blanche Wiesen Cook, *Eleanor Roosevelt, Vol. I: 1884–1933* (1992), p. 228.
42 "It wasn't just Sara . . .": Ted Morgan, *FDR: A Biography* (1985), p. 208.
42 James recalled . . . : Joseph P. Lash, *Love Eleanor: Eleanor Roosevelt and Her Friends* (1982), pp. 71–72.
42 Eleanor's cousin . . . : Morgan, p. 70.
43 "He emerged . . .": Lois Schraf, *Eleanor Roosevelt: First Lady of American Liberalism* (1987), p. 56.
43 "I have the memory . . ."; "Psyche, . . ." Ward, pp. 415–16.

CHAPTER 6

PAGE

45 Information on Rutherfurd ancestry comes from New Jersey Historical Society, Manuscript 398.
46 "years of struggle, . . .": Winthrop Rutherfurd's obituary, *New York Times*, March 21, 1944.
48 "While he [Lewis Morris Rutherfurd] . . .": ibid.
48 "He belonged . . .": ibid.
48 "Poor old Elliott . . .": *Correspondence of Theodore Roosevelt and Henry Cabot Lodge 1884–1918*, Vol. I, Henry Cabot Lodge, Ed. (1925), p. 46.
48 "breathtaking good looks . . ."; "the prototype . . .": James Brough, *Consuelo: Portrait of an American Heiress* (1979), p. 58.
49 William K. had married . . .": Jerry E. Patterson, *The Vanderbilts* (1989), pp. 120–21.
49 "I always do everything. . .": ibid.
51 "Why my parents ever. . .": Consuelo Vanderbilt Balsan, *The Glitter & the Gold* (1953), p. 23.
51 "It was in such an atmosphere . . .": ibid.

51 On board *The Valiant* . . . : Gail Maccoll Jarrett, et al., *To Marry an English Lord* (1989), p. 152.
51 "what discomfort . . .": Balsan, p. 24.
52 "I was the first woman . . .": Arthur T. Vanderbilt II, *Fortune's Children: The Fall of the House of Vanderbilt* (1989), p. 149.
52 Alva was far too busy . . . : Jarrett, et al., p. 155.
52 "none of them . . .": Balsan, p. 31.
52 Her daughter would marry . . . : Vanderbilt II, p. 148.
53 "Nothing on looks . . .": Jarrett, et al., p. 154.
53 "I felt relief . . .": Balsan, pp. 32–33.
54 "looked like an English peer . . .": Elizabeth Shoumatoff, *FDR's Unfinished Portrait* (1990), p. 75.
55 Alva was so fearful . . . : Jarrett, et al., p. 166–67.
55 Consuelo's marriage to Sunny . . . : Balsan, p. 149.
56 By 1926, Marlborough . . . : ibid., p. 192.
56 "Yes, some thirty years ago . . ." Winthrop Rutherfurd obituary, *New York Times*, March 21, 1944.

CHAPTER 7

PAGE

57 Information on the Mortons from Jonathan Daniels, *Washington Quadrille* (1968), pp. 163–68.
58 "from among her friends . . .": Consuelo Vanderbilt Balsan, *The Glitter & the Gold* (1953), p. 41.
58 Edith's sister Helen . . . : Elizabeth Eliot, *Heiresses and Coronets* (1959), p. 256.
59 Information on the Eustis family from Barbara Dombrowski, *A History of Oatlands* (1999).
59 Winthrop and Alice . . . : Winthrop Rutherfurd obituary, *New York Times*, March 21, 1944.
59 Alice's death . . . : Daniels, p. 172, and Jonathan Daniels, *The End of Innocence* (1954), p. 309.
60 "Did not Miss M . . .": p. 158.
61 "She married Mr. Rutherfurd, . . .": Daniels, *Quadrille*, p. 191.
61 Lucy phoned a mutual friend . . . : Geoffrey C. Ward, *A First-Class Temperament* (1989), p. 479.
61 "Mrs. Carroll Mercer . . .": Mercer-Rutherfurd wedding, *Washington Post*, February 14, 1920.

NOTES FOR PAGES 62–68

62 "Mr. and Mrs. Rutherfurd . . .": *New York Times*, February 11, 1920.

62 "without resources . . .": Minnie Mercer Pension File, FDRL.

62 "failed to tell . . .": Daniels, *Quadrille*, p. 190.

62 "Did you know . . .": Blanche Wiesen Cook, *Eleanor Roosevelt, Vol. I: 1884–1933* (1992), p. 229.

63 He changed his Sunday . . . : ibid., p. 228 and pp. 232–22.

63 "I wonder now . . .": ibid., pp. 249–250.

63 "Once you're elected . . .": Robert D. Graff and Robert Emmett Ginna, *F.D.R.* (1962), p. 46.

64 Information on FDR after the 1920 election from Frank Freidel, *Franklin D. Roosevelt: A Rendezvous with Destiny* (1990), pp. 39–41.

65 "I tried to persuade myself . . .": ibid., p. 41.

65 "By the end of . . .": Hugh Gregory Gallagher, *FDR's Splendid Deception* (1985), p. 10.

65 The Boston specialist . . . : Freidel, p. 42.

65 "had no real rest. . .": Eleanor Roosevelt, *This Is My Story* (1937), pp. 328–30.

65 Roosevelt and Daniels . . . : Freidel, p. 38.

66 "a trial by fire . . .": Eleanor Roosevelt, *The Autobiography of Eleanor Roosevelt* (1958), p. 114.

66 The vigorous massages . . . : Gallagher, pp. 11–13.

66 "in utter despair . . .": Freidel, p. 43.

66 "His legs . . .": ibid.

66 "Father was unbelievably . . .": James Roosevelt and Sidney Schalett, *Affectionately, FDR: A Son's Story of a Lonely Man* (1959), p. 143.

66 "out of sight . . .": Roosevelt, *Autobiography*, p. 117.

67 "sobbed and sobbed . . .": Roosevelt, *This Is My Story*, pp. 313–15.

67 "I believe that he . . .": James Roosevelt and Bill Libby, *My Parents: A Differing View* (1976), p. 95.

67 If paralytic patients . . . : Gallagher, pp. 29–30.

67 "Mother told us . . .": Anna Roosevelt, "How Polio Helped Father," *The Woman*, July 1949.

68 "I'm not going . . .": Gallagher, p. 23.

68 "walking without . . ." Freidel, p. 43.

68 "I never in my life . . .": James Roosevelt and Billy Libby, *My Parents*, p. 93.

CHAPTER 8

PAGE

69 "Back of tranquility . . .": Eleanor Roosevelt, *This Is My Story* (1937), p. 363.

70 Information on Allamuchy from Allamuchy Township.

70 Winty's kennels . . . : Jonathan Daniels, *The Washington Quadrille* (1968), pp. 209–10.

70 Information on Lucy and her gardening is from a confidential source.

71 Information on Aiken, South Carolina from the Aiken Chamber of Commerce.

72 "Lived on Yankees . . .": *A Splendid Time*, Ed. Wilkins Byrd (2000), pp. 55 and 108.

73 "I cannot help it if . . .": Evalyn Walsh McLean, *Father Struck it Rich* (1996).

73 Mrs. McLean once phoned . . . : *A Splendid Time*, p. 32.

74 Information on Eulalie Salley, Wesley Pruden, Jr., "Home-Town View on Lucy-FDR: It Can't Be True," *The National Observer*, August, 1966.

74 Five fire companies . . . : *New York Times*, June 8, 1939.

75 Gussie Gardner . . . : Frank Freidel, *Franklin D. Roosevelt: A Rendezvous with Destiny* (1990), pp. 28–29.

75 Ridgely Hall . . . : *A Splendid Time*, p. 44 and 110.

75 Aiken saw Winty . . . : Pruden, August, 1966.

76 "When I was 17 . . .": Anna Halsted Papers, Box 84, Folder 1, FDRL.

76 Letter from Lucy Mercer Rutherfurd to FDR, April 16, 1927, Roosevelt Family Papers Donated by the Children, Box 21, Folder 10, FDRL.

77 She called him "lazy, selfish . . .": ER to SDR, February 8, 1919, *FDR: His Personal Letters*, Ed. Elliott Roosevelt, Vol. 2, p. 467.

78 "No movies . . .": Freidel, p. 47.

78 So successful was he . . . : Hugh Gregory Gallagher, *FDR's Splendid Deception* (1985), p. xiii.

CHAPTER 9

PAGE

79 "How is the farm? . . .": Confidential source.

81 Franklin Roosevelt as governor . . . : Frank Freidel, *Franklin D. Roosevelt: A Rendezvous with Destiny* (1990), pp. 58–61.

81 "a new deal . . .": ibid., p. 73.
81 Roosevelt's "whistle-stop," Friedel, pp. 77–78.
82 "In one week . . .": Rebecca Brooks Gruver, *An American History* (1978), pp. 452–53.
83 White House aide . . . : Raymond Moley, *The First New Deal* (1966), pp. 273–75.
83 "Though she did not . . .": Eleanor Roosevelt, *This I Remember* (1937), p. 28.
84 "All wander around . . .": *FDR: His Personal Letters*, Ed. Elliott Roosevelt, Vol. II, March 5, 1923.
84 "seemed eerie . . .": Roosevelt, *This I Remember*, pp. 345–46.
84 As with Warm Springs . . . : Grace Tully, *F.D.R., My Boss* (1949), pp. 23–24.
85 "There were days . . ."; "F.D. . . .": Geoffrey C. Ward, *A First Class Temperament* (1989), pp. 676–79.
85 "She watches her man . . .": ibid., p. 711.
85 "had had rheumatic fever . . .": Roosevelt, *This I Remember*, p. 28.
85 "I think she has . . .": Ward, p. 714.
85 "Don't you ever . . .": Joseph P. Lash, *Eleanor Roosevelt: A Friend's Memoir* (1964), p. 210.
86 Anna called her . . . : Ward, p. 713.
86 "I believe there may have been . . .": James Roosevelt and Bill Libby, *My Parents: A Differing View* (1976), pp. 110–11.
86 Miller later admitted . . . : Joseph P. Lash, *Eleanor and Franklin: The Story of Their Relationship* (1971), pp. 117–19.
86 Lillian Rogers Parks . . . : Lillian Rogers Parks with Spatz Leighton, *The Roosevelts: A Family in Turmoil* (1981), p. 185.
87 As a society matron of Aiken . . . : Earl Miller to the Abelows, August, 22, 1966, FDRL.
87 "Father encouraged it, . . .": James Roosevelt, p. 107.
87 "How could anyone . . .": Doris Kearns Goodwin, *No Ordinary Time* (1994), p. 154.
88 "After his forced break with Lucy . . .": James Roosevelt, p. 104.
88 "no background at all . . .": Bernard Asbell, *The FDR Memoirs* (1973), p. 247.
88 "Father, I think, . . .": James Roosevelt, p. 105.
88 "Missy was the only woman . . .": Ward, p. 710.
88 "Mr. President . . .": confidential source
89 "This great nation will endure . . .": Nathan Miller, *FDR: An Intimate History* (1963), p. 306.

89 "Livy's death . . .": Elliott Roosevelt, Ed., *FDR: His Personal Letters*, Vol. 1 (1947), p. 24.

89 Livy left his old friend . . . : *New York Times*, January 14, 1932.

89 Information on Lucy's nephew is from a confidential source.

89 Roosevelt assassination attempt by Zangara from Freidel, pp. 87–88.

CHAPTER 10

PAGE

91 Information on Lucy and Rutherfurd comes from a confidential source.

92 Information on Aiken, S.C. comes from the Aiken Historical Society and issues of the Aiken *Standard and Review* from the 1930s and 1940s.

92 "Lucy, I have just heard . . .": Jonathan Daniels, *Washington Quadrille* (1968), p. 251.

93 Information on The Willcox Inn, Gwen Thurmond, "The Willcox Inn," *South Carolina Smiles*, publication by South Carolina Department of Parks, Recreation and Tourism.

93 "All five stepchildren . . ."; "I can truly say . . .": Elizabeth Shoumatoff, *FDR's Unfinished Portrait* (1990), pp. 75–77.

94 Lucy deferred her portrait . . .": ibid.

94 "He was the object of constant care . . .": ibid., p. 76.

94 For Shoumatoff . . . : ibid., pp. 76–79.

95 Her orders were . . . : Geoffrey C. Ward, *A First-Class Temperament* (1989), p. 777.

95 Letter from Lucy to FDR, 1940, FDRL.

97 The record of "Mrs. Johnson's" visits to the White House from the Usher's Diary. Bernard Asbell interviewed Secret Service agent William D. Simmons for his book *The FDR Memoirs* (1973), p. 411.

97 Times and dates of visits to Missy LeHand from White House Log, FDRL.

97 "when to approach . . .": article on Marguerite LeHand from *Saturday Evening Post*, January 8, 1938.

98 "Nothing is more pleasing . . ." James Roosevelt and Bill Libby, *My Parents: A Differing View* (1976), p. 17.

98 "exactly as a princess . . .": Bess Furman, *Washington By-Line* (1949), p. 288.

99 "anyone was her social equal . . ." Doris Kearns Goodwin, *No Ordinary Time* (1994), p. 153.

99 "the president's girlfriend . . .": ibid.

100 "a little crackup . . ."; "a nervous breakdown . . .": Bernard Asbell, *The FDR Memoirs* (1973), p. 241.

100 "Don't you dare . . .": Ward, p. 792.

101 "the strain of loving . . .": Lillian Rogers Parks with Spatz Leighton, *The Roosevelts: A Family in Turmoil* (1981), pp. 186–87.

101 Missy refused all visitors . . . : Bernard Asbell, *Mother and Daughter: The Letters of Eleanor and Anna Roosevelt* (1988), p. 133.

102 For Elliott Roosevelt, . . . : Goodwin, p. 245.

102 "He missed Missy . . .": James Roosevelt and Bill Libby, *My Parents: A Differing View* (1976), p. 109.

102 "She served me so well . . ."; and information on Roosevelt's will . . . : ibid., p. 108.

102 FDR's will, November 12, 1941, FDRL.

CHAPTER 11

PAGE

104 "ask that every American . . .": Fireside Chat, September 3, 1939, FDRL.

104 "Never in the field of human conflict . . .": Tribute to Royal Air Force, House of Commons, August, 1940.

104 "peace in our time . . .": Address from 10 Downing St. after return from Munich Conference.

105 "In the future days . . .": *New York Times*, January 7, 1941.

105 Days and times of Lucy's White House visits from White House Usher's Diary, FDRL.

106 "It was awfully nice . . ."; In July 19, 1942 . . . : Anna R. Halsted Papers, Box 70, Folder 5, FDRL.

106 Information on FDR's and Lucy's outings from Jonathan Daniels, *Washington Quadrille* (1968), p. 296 and a confidential source.

107 "peace of mind . . .": FDR to SDR, July 24, 1941, Box 10, Ross Family Papers Donated by the Children, FDRL.

107 "When my son comes . . .": Geoffrey C. Ward, *A First-Class Temperament* (1989), p. 3.

107 Information on the death of Sara Roosevelt from Rita Halle Kleeman, *Gracious Lady: The Life of Sara Delano Roosevelt* (1935), p. 233.

107 "struck, as we all were, . . .": Michael F. Reilly, *Reilly of the White House* (1947), p. 84.

108 "The loss of a brother . . .": Eleanor Roosevelt, *This I Remember* (1949), p. 228.

108 "I looked at my mother-in-law's face . . .": Joseph. P. Lash, *Eleanor and Franklin: The Story of Their Relationship* (1971), pp. 642–43.

108 Following her funeral, . . . : Grace Tully, *F.D.R., My Boss* (1949), p. 105.

108 Information on Minna Mercer from Minna Mercer Pension File, FDRL and a confidential source.

109 Information on the Pearl Harbor attack from Frank Freidel, *Franklin D. Roosevelt: A Rendezvous with Destiny* (1990), pp. 405–06.

110 "Yesterday comma . . .": Tully, p. 256.

110 "very strained and tired . . ."; "But he was . . .": Eleanor Roosevelt interview, Graff Papers, FDRL.

110 "the fate of all that is good . . .": Lucy to FDR, 1940, FDRL.

CHAPTER 12

PAGE

111 "To have the United States . . .": Winston Churchill, *The Second World War, Vol. III, The Grand Alliance* (1950), p. 538.

112 The war put great demands . . . : Doris Kearns Goodwin, *No Ordinary Time* (1994), p. 624.

112 Information on Rosie from www.rosietheriveter.org.

112 "By December 7, 1941, . . .": James Roosevelt and Bill Libby, *My Parents: A Differing View* (1976), p. 266.

112 Roosevelt's telegrams to Barbara from file on Lucy Rutherfurd, FDRL.

113 Information on Rutherfurds in the military from President's secretary's file on Rutherfurd family, Box 164, FDRL and file on Lucy Rutherfurd, FDRL.

113 "be nice . . ."; "because Father . . .": Anna Roosevelt Halsted, unpublished manuscript, Anna Roosevelt Halsted Papers, Box 84, Folder 1, FDRL.

113 Roosevelt had also supplied . . . : Grace Tully, *F.D.R., My Boss* (1949), p. 328.

114 "For more than five hundred days—": *New York Times*, May 19, 1943.

114 "There was a war . . .": Joseph P. Lash, *Love Eleanor: Eleanor Roosevelt and Her Friends* (1982), p. 66.

114 "my miseries reminded . . .": Anna Roosevelt Halsted, review of Joseph P. Lash, *Eleanor Roosevelt: A Friend's Memoir*, Box 36, Halsted Papers, FDRL.

115 Information on Eleanor Roosevelt and Val-Kill from Eleanor Roosevelt Historic Site, New York.

116 Information on Lorena Hickok from Blanche Wiesen Cook, *Eleanor Roosevelt, Vol, I: 1884–1933* (1992), pp. 477–78.

117 "Oh! I want to put . . .": ER to Lorena Hickok, March 7, 1933, Hickok Papers, FDRL.

117 "obvious to some servants . . .": Lillian Rogers Parks with Spatz Leighton, *The Roosevelts: A Family in Turmoil* (1981), p. 5.

117 "Every woman wants . . .": Joseph P. Lash, *A World of Love: Eleanor Roosevelt and Her Friends, 1943–1962* (1984), 116.

117 "You taught me more . . .": ibid., p. 211.

118 Hick left the Associated Press . . . : Doris Faber, *The Life of Lorena Hickok: E.R.'s Friend* (1980), pp. 278–79.

118 When Roosevelt came home . . .": Geoffrey C. Ward, *A First-Class Temperament* (1989), pp. 140–41.

119 Information on Shoumatoff painting FDR at the White House from Elizabeth Shoumatoff, *FDR's Unfinished Portrait* (1990), pp. 80–82 and 87–90.

120 "I am alone . . .": confidential source.

CHAPTER 13

PAGE

121 "Absolutely no women, . . .": Joseph. P. Lash, *A World of Love: Eleanor Roosevelt and Her Friends, 1943–1962* (1982), p. 93.

121 "I've been amused . . .": ibid., p. 96.

121 Anna forgave . . . : Anna Roosevelt Boettiger to John Boettiger, Dec. 27, 1943, Box 6, Boettiger Papers, FDRL.

122 "See who's home . . .": Nathan Miller, *FDR, An Intimate History* (1983), p. 493.

122 "that touch of triviality . . .": Joseph P. Lash, *Eleanor and Franklin: The Story of Their Relationship* (1971), p. 699.

122 "Father could relax . . .": Doris Kearns Goodwin, *No Ordinary Time* (1994), p. 489.

122 "I found myself trying . . .": John R. Boettiger, Jr., *A Love in Shadow* (1978), p. 253.

122 "She personally would love it, . . .": Lash, *Eleanor and Franklin*, p. 699.

123 "This would annoy . . .": Bernard Asbell, *Mother and Daughter: The Letters of Eleanor and Anna Roosevelt* (1988), p. 99.

123 "Sis, you handle that, . . .": ibid., pp. 175–76.

123 "ideal match, . . .": Goodwin, p. 419.

123 "young life . . .": Eleanor Roosevelt, "My Day," March 4, 1944.

123 "She is a wonderful person . . .": Geoffrey C. Ward, Ed. *Closest Companion: The Unknown Story of the Intimate Friendship between Franklin Roosevelt and Margaret Suckley* (1995), p. 284.

123 "really knew what . . .": Asbell, *Mother and Daughter*, p. 177.

124 ". . .he hopes to show her . . .": ibid., p. 287.

124 "I suspected something was . . .": Goodwin, 494.

124 "There was then no specific . . ." *Closest Companion*, p. 289.

124 "The president can't take . . .": Bert E. Park, M.D., *Ailing, Aging, Addicted: Studies of Compromised Leadership* (1993), p. 194.

125 "I don't think Mother . . ."; "the weariness . . .": Asbell, *Mother and Daughter*, p. 177.

125 "He is . . .": Ward, *Closest Companion*, p. 297.

125 "I want to sleep . . .": Bernard Baruch, *Baruch: The Public Years* (1960), pp. 335–37.

126 "I came home . . .": Eleanor Roosevelt, *This I Remember* (1949), p. 328.

126 On April 28, Lucy . . . : Bernard Asbell, *The FDR Memoirs* (1973), p. 412.

126 "What would you think . . .": Goodwin, p. 517.

127 Over the next nine months, . . . : Geoffrey C. Ward, *A First-Class Temperament* (1989), p. 777.

127 "By this time he was . . .": James Roosevelt with Bill Libby, *My Parents: A Differing View* (1976), p. 103.

127 "clandestine about these . . .": Anna Roosevelt Halstead Papers, Box 84, Folder 1, FDRL.

128 "I remember feeling happy . . ." ibid.

128 "Never did Father and I . . ." ibid.

128 Alonzo Fields, . . . : Goodwin, p. 520.

128 The next day Franklin and Lucy . . . : Jonathan Daniels, *Washington Quadrille* (1968), pp. 297–98.

129 "[T]he strength of his beloved presence—": Lucy to Anna Roosevelt Boettiger, May 9, 1945, Box 70, Halstead Papers, FDRL.

129 "You and I lost . . .": Asbell, *FDR Memoirs*, p. 404.

130 "Mrs. Roosevelt and I send . . .": Ward, *A First-Class Temperament*, p. 776.

130 Information on Roosevelt's trip to Allamuchy: Goodwin, p. 52 and Shoumatoff p. 108.

131 After Roosevelt's death, Lucy admitted . . . : Joseph Alsop, *FDR: A Centenary Remembrance* (1982), p. 68.

131 Daisy Suckley noted in her diary . . . : Ward, Ed. *Closest Companion*, pp. 323–24.

132 "Told the president . . .": William D. Hassett, *Off the Record with F.D.R.* (1958), p. 269.

133 After the president had left, . . . : Bob Withers, *The President Travels by Train* (1966), p. 176.

133 They sat on the porch . . . : Ward, Ed., *Closest Companion*, p. 325.

CHAPTER 14

PAGE

134 Information on Laura "Polly" Delano from Geoffrey C.Ward, Ed., *Closest Companion: The Unknown Story of the Intimate Friendship between Franklin Roosevelt and Margaret Suckley* (1995), pp. 20–21.

135 "Daisy was as homey . . .": Elliott Roosevelt and James Brough, *An Untold Story: The Roosevelts of Hyde Park* (1973), p. 281.

135 "my part of prim spinster . . .": Ward, Ed., *Closest Companion*, pp. xi–xiii.

135 "These Republican leaders . . .": Franklin D. Roosevelt, *Public Papers and Addresses of Franklin D. Roosevelt, 1941–1945*, 4 vols., Samuel I. Rosenman, Ed. (1950), p. 290.

136 "the greatest little ham . . .": Michael F. Reilly, *Reilly of the White House* (1947), p. 63.

136 "You're the only people . . .": Geoffrey C. Ward, *A First-Class Temperament* (1989), p. 629..

136 "Laura Delano had no . . .": Roosevelt and Brough, *An Untold Story*, p. 281.

136 Daisy described Lucy, . . . : Ward, Ed., *Closest Companion*, p. 351.

136 Daisy's details of Lucy and Barbara's Warm Springs visit from Ward, Ed., *Closest Companion*, pp. 349–353.

137 "As Lucy said all this . . .": Bernard Asbell, *Mother and Daughter: The Letters of Eleanor and Anna Roosevelt* (1988), p. 187.

138 A week later Lucy . . . : Ward, Ed., *Closest Companion*, pp. 358–59.

138 The president left . . . : ibid., p. 365.

138 On January 12, 1945 . . . : ibid., p. 380.

138 "Who is there here . . .": Samuel I. Rosenman, *Working with Roosevelt* (1952), p. 516.

138 "Dog catchers . . .": Reilly, p. 516.

139 James Roosevelt had come . . . : James Roosevelt with Bill Libby, *My Parents: A Differing View* (1976), p. 283.

139 The brief ceremonies . . . : Frank Freidel, *Franklin D. Roosevelt: A Rendezvous with Destiny* (1989), pp. 573–74.

139 "It would look bad . . .": James Roosevelt, p. 283.

139 "That conversation . . .": ibid., p. 284.

140 Daisy recorded . . . : Ward, Ed., *Closest Companion*, pp. 387–88.

140 "over there is where . . .": Anna Roosevelt Halsted Papers, Box 84, Folder 1, FDRL.

140 "a lot of little gadgets . . .": Anna Roosevelt Boettiger to John Boettiger, Feb. 6, 1945, Box 6, Boettiger Papers, FDRL and Ward, Ed., *Closest Companion*, p. 385.

141 "One of the world's . . .": Ward, Ed., *Closest Companion*, pp. 394–95.

141 "I am really worried . . .": ibid., 395.

141 "To a doctor's eye, . . .": *Churchill—The Struggle for Survival, 1940–1965: Taken from the Diaries of Lord Moran* (1966), p. 242.

141 He asked the Congress . . . : Rosenman, p. 527.

142 "There was somebody . . .": Elizabeth Shoumatoff, *FDR's Unfinished Portrait* (1990), p. 98.

142 "I am glad that the trip . . .": Ward, Ed., *Closest Companion*, p. 402.

143 "We will leave . . .": Shoumatoff, p. 100.

143 Due to poor directions: ibid., p. 101.

CHAPTER 15

PAGE

144 Eleanor Roosevelt's account of FDR's death from Eleanor Roosevelt, *This I Remember* (1949), pp. 343–44.

NOTES FOR PAGES 145–152

145 "Harry, the President . . .": Harry Truman, *Memoirs. Vol. I: Year of Decisions* (1955), p. 5.

145 "I felt like the moon, . . .": ibid., p. 19.

145 "I never really thought . . .": Michael F. Reilly, *Reilly of the White House* (1947), p. 226.

145 "It was a malicious . . .": Bernard Asbell, *Mother and Daughter: The Letters of Eleanor and Anna Roosevelt* (1988), p. 186.

146 "Eleanor would have found . . .": Jim Bishop, *FDR's Last Year* (1974), p. 635.

146 "Her eyes were dry . . .": Grace Tully, *F.D.R., My Boss* (1949), p. 366.

146 "Mother was so upset . . ."; "It was all . . .": Anna Boettiger notes attached to letter to Joseph Lash, January 28, 1972, Box 36, Halsted Papers, FDRL.

146 "Mother was angry . . ." James Roosevelt with Bill Libby, *My Parents: A Differing View* (1976), pp. 103–04.

147 "Thank you so very . . .": Lucy Rutherfurd to Eleanor Roosevelt, May 2, 1945, Eleanor Roosevelt Papers, FDRL.

147 Lucy's letter to Anna: Lucy Rutherfurd to Anna Roosevelt Boettiger, May 9, 1945, Box 70, Halsted Papers, FDRL.

148 Details of Lucy and Daisy's relationship following FDR's death and Lucy's visit to his grave from Daisy's daybook for June 9, 1945 and Lucy's letters to Daisy: May 9, 1945, May 20, 1945, June 19, 1945, Margaret Suckley Papers, Wilderstein Preservation.

150 She had loved Winty, . . . : Joseph Alsop, *A Centenary Remembrance* (1982), p. 68.

150 "It must have been Franklin . . .": Ted Morgan, *FDR: A Biography* (1985), p. 207.

151 Details of Lucy's later years from Jonathan Daniels, *Washington Quadrille* (1968), pp. 317–323.

151 Details of Minna Mercer's death from the Minna Mercer Pension File, FDRL.

152 "Grace Tully wired me . . .": Anna Boettiger to Daisy Suckley, October 25, 1948, FDRL.

152 The story of Lucy and purchasing the flowers and vegetables is from a confidential source.

BIBLIOGRAPHY

Alsop, Joseph. *FDR: A Centenary Remembrance*. New York: Viking, 1982.

Asbell, Bernard. *The FDR Memoirs*. Garden City, NY: Doubleday, 1973.

———. *Mother and Daughter: The Letters of Eleanor and Anna Roosevelt*. New York: Fromm, 1988.

———. *When F.D.R. Died*. New York: Holt, Rinehart & Winston, 1961.

Balsan, Consuelo Vanderbilt. *The Glitter & the Gold*. Maidstone, Kent: George Mann Books, 1953.

Bishop, Jim. *FDR's Last Year*. New York: William Morrow, 1974.

Boettiger, John R., Jr. *A Love in Shadow*. New York: Norton, 1978.

Brough, James. *Consuelo: Portrait of an American Heiress*. New York: Coward, McCann & Geoghegan, 1979.

Byrd, Wilkins, Ed. *A Splendid Time: Photographs of Old Aiken*. Aiken, SC: The Historic Aiken Foundation, 2000.

Caroli, Betty Boyd. *The Roosevelt Women*. New York: Basic Books, 1998.

Churchill, Winston S. *The Second World War*. Vol. 3., *The Grand Alliance*. Boston: Houghton Mifflin, 1950.

Cook, Blanche Wiesen. *Eleanor Roosevelt, Vol. 1, 1884–1933*, New York: Penguin Books, 1992.

———. *Eleanor Roosevelt, Vol. 2, 1933–1938*. New York: Penguin Books, 1999.

Daniels, Jonathan. *The Time between the Wars*. Garden City, NY: Doubleday, 1966.

———. *Washington Quadrille: The Dance beside the Documents*. Garden City, NY: Doubleday, 1968.

Davis, Kenneth S. *FDR: The Beckoning of Destiny, 1882–1928*. New York: Putnam, 1971.

Dombrowski, Barbara. *A History of Oatlands*. Leesburg, VA: Oatlands, Inc., 1999.

Eliot, Elizabeth. *Heiresses and Coronets: The Story of Lovely Ladies and Noble Men*. New York: McDowell, Obolensky, 1959.

Faber, Doris. *The Life of Lorena Hickok: E. R.'s Friend*. New York: Morrow, 1980.

Freidel, Frank. *Franklin D. Roosevelt: A Rendevous with Destiny*. Boston: Little, Brown, 1990.

Furman, Bess. *Washington By-Line*. New York: Knopf, 1949.

Gallagher, Hugh Gregory. *FDR's Splendid Deception*. New York: Dodd, Mead, 1985.

Goodwin, Doris Kearns. *No Ordinary Time, Franklin and Eleanor Roosevelt: The Home Front in World War II*. New York: Simon & Schuster, 1994.

Gruver, Rebecca. *An American History*. Reading, MA: Addison-Wesley, 1978.

Hassett, William D. *Off the Record with F.D.R.* New Brunswick, NJ: Rutgers University Press, 1958.

Jarrett, Gail Maccoll, et al. *To Marry an English Lord*. New York: Workman, 1989.

Kleeman, Rita Halle. *Gracious Lady: The Life of Sara Delano Roosevelt*. New York: Appleton-Century, 1935.

Lash, Joseph P. *Eleanor Roosevelt: A Friend's Memoir*. Garden City, NY: Doubleday, 1964.

———. *Eleanor and Franklin: The Story of Their Relationship*. New York: Norton, 1971.

———. *Love Eleanor: Eleanor Roosevelt and Her Friends*. Garden City, NY: Doubleday, 1982.

———. *A World of Love: Eleanor Roosevelt and Her Friends, 1932–1962*. Garden City, NY: Doubleday, 1984.

"Marguerite LeHand." *Saturday Evening Post*, January 8, 1938.

Lippman, Theo, Jr., *The Squire of Warm Springs: FDR in Georgia, 1924–1945*. Chicago: Playboy Press, 1977.

Lodge, Henry Cabot, *Correspondence of Theodore Roosevelt and Henry Cabot Lodge 1884–1918*, Vol. 1, Henry Cabot Lodge, Ed., 1925.

Mares, Franklin D. *Springwood*. Hyde Park, NY: Hyde Park Historical Association, 1993.

McLean, Evalyn Walsh. *Father Struck It Rich*. Cheshire Moon Publications, 1996.

Miller, Nathan. *FDR, An Intimate History*. Garden City, NY: Doubleday, 1983.

Moley, Raymond. *The First New Deal*. New York: Harcourt, Brace and World, 1966.

BIBLIOGRAPHY

Moran, Lord. *Churchill—The Struggle for Survival, 1940–1965: Taken from the Diaries of Lord Moran*. Boston: Houghton Mifflin, 1966.

Morgan, Ted. *FDR: A Biography*. New York: Simon & Schuster, 1985.

Park, Bert E. *Ailing, Aging, Addicted: Studies of Compromised Leadership*. Lexington: University Press of Kentucky, 1993.

Parks, Lillian Rogers with Francis Spatz Leighton. *The Roosevelts: A Family in Turmoil*. Englewood, NJ: Fleet, 1981.

Patterson, Jerry E. *The Vanderbilts*. New York: Henry N. Abrams, 1989.

Pruden, Wesley. "Home Town View On Lucy-FDR: It Can't Be True," *The National Observer*, August, 1966.

Reilly, Michael F. *Reilly of the White House*. New York: Simon & Schuster, 1947.

Roosevelt, Anna. "How Polio Helped Father," *The Woman*, July 1949.

Roosevelt, Eleanor. *The Autobiography of Eleanor Roosevelt*. New York: Harper & Row, 1958, 1978: New York: G. K. Hall, 1984.

———. *This I Remember*. New York: Harper & Brothers, 1949.

———. *This Is My Story*. New York: Harper, 1937.

Roosevelt, Elliott and James Brough. *An Untold Story: The Roosevelts of Hyde Park*. New York: Putnam, 1973.

Roosevelt, Franklin D. *FDR: His Personal Letters, Vol. 1, The Early Years*. Edited by Elliott Roosevelt. New York: Duell, Sloan & Pearce, 1947.

———. *FDR: His Personal Letters, Vol. II*. Edited by Elliott Roosevelt. New York: Duell, Sloan & Pearce, 1947.

———. *Public Papers and Addresses of Franklin D. Roosevelt, 1941–1945*. 4 vols, edited by Samuel I. Rosenman. New York: Harper, 1950.

Roosevelt, James with Bill Libby. *My Parents: A Differing View*. Chicago: Playboy Press, 1976.

Roosevelt, James and Sidney Schalett, *Affectionately, F.D.R.: A Son's Story of a Lonely Man*. New York: Harcourt, Brace, 1959.

Rosenman, Samuel I. *Working with Roosevelt*. New York: Harper, 1952.

Winthrop Rutherfurd Obituary, *New York Times*, March 21, 1944.

Scharf, Lois. *ER: First Lady of American Liberalism*. Boston: Twayne Publishers, 1987.

Shoumatoff, Elizabeth. *FDR's Unfinished Portrait*. Pittsburgh PA: University of Pittsburgh Press, 1990.

Teague, Michael. *Mrs. L: Conversations with Alice Roosevelt Longworth*. Garden City, NY: Doubleday, 1981.

"Thinks That FDR Wanted to Marry Lucy the Lovely." *The Daily News*, August 13, 1966.

Thurmond, Gwen. "Willcox Inn." *South Carolina Smiles*, South Carolina Department of Parks, Recreation and Tourism.

Truman, Harry. *Memoirs. Vol. 1: Year of Decisions*. Garden City, NY: Doubleday, 1955.

Tully, Grace. *F.D.R., My Boss*. New York: Charles Scribner's Sons, 1949.

Vanderbilt, Arthur T., II. *Fortune's Children: The Fall of the House of Vanderbilt*. New York: Perennial, 2001.

Ward, Geoffrey C., Ed., *Closest Companion: The Unknown Story of the Intimate Friendship between Franklin Roosevelt and Margaret Suckley*. Boston: Houghton Mifflin, 1995.

———. *A First-Class Temperament: The Emergence of Franklin Roosevelt*. New York: Harper & Row: 1989.

INDEX